HISTORY OF THE

GREATER

BOSTON

TRACK CLUB

PAUL C. CLERICI

Charleston — London

THE
History
PRESS

Published by The History Press
Charleston, SC 29403
www.historypress.net

Front cover, top left: Bill Squires (left) and Bill Rodgers. *Jeff Johnson photo, courtesy Bill Squires*; *top right*: Dave McGillivray. *Courtesy Dave McGillivray*; *middle*: Fred Doyle on the shoulders of British police constable Richard Raine. *Courtesy Fred Doyle*; *bottom*: The Greater Boston Track Club team at Icahn Stadium. *GreaterSnap photo, courtesy GBTC*.
Back cover, top left: Alberto Salazar. *Courtesy Bob Sevene*; *top right*: Greater Boston Track Club runners (from left) Hannah Hastings, Jenny Gardynski, Laura Hayden and Victoria Barnaby. *GreaterSnap photo, courtesy GBTC*; *bottom*: Pete Pfitzinger. *Photo by Leo Kulinski Jr.*

First published 2013

Manufactured in the United States

ISBN 978.1.62619.030.6

Library of Congress CIP data applied for.

I dedicate this book to my parents, Frank Clerici Sr. and Carol Hunt-Clerici; my brothers, Frank Clerici Jr. and the late David Clerici; and my "sisters," Regina Clerici, Beverly Jaeger and Lynn Marcus. They never fail to support me, love me and make me guffaw.

This book is also dedicated to all those affected—directly or indirectly—by the bombings at the 2013 Boston Marathon. As a running family, we mourn those whom we've lost, encourage those who are hurt and embrace all for strength and comfort. By doing this, we win the greatest race—good against evil.

Contents

Foreword, by Coach Bill Squires   7
Acknowledgements   9
Introduction   11

One: 1973–1979   13
Two: 1980–1989   61
Three: 1990–1999   91
Four: 2000–2009   99
Five: 2010–2013   109

Index   123
About the Author   128

Foreword

The Greater Boston Track Club (GBTC) was founded in 1973 and wasn't so much a distance running club in the beginning; it was more of an all-inclusive group with sprinters, hurdlers and middle-distance runners. The club was made up of athletes looking to further advance their running goals in a team atmosphere.

The phenomenal success of GBTC took place in the late 1970s into the 1980s, a success made most public when four of the top ten finishers in the 1979 Boston Marathon came from its membership. I told my runners, "You do things together that you would never do alone. You share what you have. You kick around ideas. And you succeed."

I liked to play around with training techniques, surprise my athletes, make any situation as fun as it was competitive. With the belief that repetition and familiarity are keys to success, I had my athletes doing hill workouts on Heartbreak Hill so that they'd still be able to lift their legs once they got tired and running from Boston College out to Wellesley and back along the Boston course so that they would know how to race every inch of it. A three-week training scheme would include long and short intervals and a long run with fartlek (speed variations). Whatever the exact race situation was going to be—whether on the track, cross-country or roads—I wanted my athletes to be prepared. We did [the practices] so many times, we could do [them] in our sleep. The racing schedule included a race once every third week, compared to the popular weekly or bimonthly racing schedule.

I believe in moderation on the track and that a coach needs to control where and when his athletes race. Above all, I believe in the importance of belief in oneself and in the courage to think big. As the stable of horses grew in the late 1970s, every athlete—whether put in the A, B or C group—went above and beyond his expectations. This was achieved because each runner believed he could make it to the next level and thus constantly achieved personal records (PRs). In less than two years of training with this program together with his GBTC teammates, Bill Rodgers finished third at the 1975 IAAF World Cross-Country Championships and shortly thereafter won the 1975 Boston Marathon in an American Record (AR), 2:09:55. That's when things really took off. With Rodgers as a magnet, the club quickly drew the rest of the region's top distance runners and, eventually, a few from outside New England as well. But the internal effect was more dramatic. Rodgers, after all, had run just 2:19:34 at Boston in 1974. His GBTC teammates now looked at him and said, "Wait a minute. I can hang with him in workouts. If he can run 2:09, I can run 2:11." That type of group training was what made GBTC so effective.

In 1979, Rodgers ran a course record of 2:09:27 for his third Boston victory. No one was surprised. Randy Thomas came in eighth at 2:14:12. No surprise there either. But Bob Hodge bursting forth with a sixteen-minute PR to finish in 2:12:30 for third? Dick Mahoney, a mailman, running 2:14:36 for tenth place? With four finishers in the top ten of probably the finest marathon field ever put together, the next day's newspaper said GBTC was *the* marathon club. The city honored the quartet in a ceremony at historic Faneuil Hall.

Before the success slowed in the mid-1980s due to big-name shoe companies establishing teams, GBTC would go down in history as one of the greatest amateur running clubs in the United States. On its résumé are three of the top five finishers in the 1978 Boston; four of the top ten finishers in the 1979 Boston; more than twenty national AAU titles at various distances; six consecutive U.S. 25K road-racing team titles; nine consecutive U.S. 20K titles; nine men under 14:04 in the 5,000; nine men under 29:59 in the 10,000; the 1979 Senior Men's Cross-Country team championship, in which GBTC runners were first, third, fourth, fifth and twelfth and outscored the second-place team 26–179; and in track, several indoor championships in the two-mile relay and distance medley relay, the team for which also won a national championship.

The early seeds that were planted in the GBTC runners also produced many fruits in the form of successful high school, college, track club and Olympic coaches.

COACH BILL SQUIRES
April 2013

Acknowledgements

I wish to thank Rich Benyo, David Callum, Louisa Clerici, Paul Collyer, Jack Fleming, Erin (Cullinane) Kandamar, Andrew Kastor, Tim Kilduff, Maurice Kornreich, Leo Kulinski Jr., Bob Levitsky, Doug McLucas, Frank Monkiewicz, Dennis O'Rourke, Kathy Rolfe, Jeff Saraceno, Jan Seeley, Bill Squires Jr., Priscilla Squires, Fred Treseler, Julia Turner, Kit Wells and Andy Yelenak. Additional thanks goes to those who graciously gave of their time for interviews: Jon Berit, Ben Bosworth, Lois Brommer Duquette, Gary Circosta, Nancy Clark, Norma Deprospo, Dan Dillon, Pam Duckworth, Stanley Egbor, Kyle Linn MacQueen Feldman, Dotty Fine, Jack Fultz, Sharon (O'Hagan) Gilligan, Thom Gilligan, Tom Grilk, Bob Hall, Laura Hayden, Jim Hebert, Bob Hodge, Israel Horovitz, Johann Jack, Sebastian Junger, Ann King, Chris Lane, Pat (Meade) Lavelle, Tommy Leonard, Dick Mahoney, Allison McCabe, Jack McDonald, Kay McDonald, Dave McGillivray, John McGrath, Greg Meyer, Ioannis Papadopolous, Jim Pawlicki, Pete Pfitzinger, Kirk Pfrangle, Toni Reavis, Don Ricciato, Bill Rodgers, Amory Rowe Salem, Alberto Salazar, Bob Sevene, Jean Smith, Gary Snyder, Bill Squires, Randy Thomas and Anna Willard. For further assistance and interviews, I thank Tom Derderian, Fred Doyle, Mark Duggan, Cynthia Hastings and John Raguin. And for research, I thank ARRS (Association of Road Racing Statisticians), Athlinks, Bill Rodgers Running Center, BAA (Boston Athletic Association), Boston College Athletics, Boston University Athletics, Bob Hodge Running Page, coolrunning, Endicott College Athletics, Falmouth Road Race, Globe Santa, Greater Boston Track Club, the *Harvard Crimson*,

Acknowledgements

Harvard University Athletics, IAAF (International Association of Athletics Federations), *Marathon & Beyond*, MarathonGuide, Masters Track and Field, Oceana Athletics Association, *Pittsburgh Post-Gazette*, Providence College Athletics, RRCA (Road Runners Club of America), *Runner's World*, Twin Cities in Motion, United Kingdom Athletics, University of Minnesota Athletics and USATF (United States of America Track & Field).

Introduction

In some ways, the history of the Greater Boston Track Club reads like a person's life story. There was the birth, growing pains, meeting of relatives, great times, sad times, difficult times, growth spurts, adulthood, new kids, deaths and more births. And it still looks great at forty.

The *History of the Greater Boston Track Club* had a gestation period of about four months from creation to completion. Talk began shortly after Bill Squires's eightieth birthday celebration at Boston College in November 2012, when several hundred people—including many former and current GBTC members—gathered to honor the club's first coach. In January 2013, research, interviews and writing began in earnest. My enjoyment of immersing myself in GBTC's forty years was matched only by the sharing of stories and tales from those who lived it. As someone who has run races from the mile to the marathon, I have often seen and talked with GBTC athletes at these and other events. It was a complete joy being surrounded by so much positive energy from these athletes, whether at a race, in an e-mail or over the phone.

The most difficult aspect for me, personally, was to not run in the 2013 Boston Marathon. For twenty-three consecutive years—from 1990 to 2012—I had taken that annual Patriots' Day holiday trip to Hopkinton and run eastward for 26.2 miles until I reached the beautiful and welcoming arm of the downtown Boston finish line. I celebrated, suffered, loved and enjoyed every second of it, especially those final few minutes, when I was cheered on by my family from the bleacher seats just before the finish. With no regrets, this book was the reason I chose not to run. In order for the book to be released in time for GBTC's fortieth anniversary in August 2013, the publisher's deadline was May 1, 2013, a mere sixteen days after Boston. I soon realized back in January that I could not properly train for Boston and thoroughly write this book.

While I was in Boston on a separate writing assignment earlier on Marathon Monday, my family and I were home and witnessed on TV when the horror of the bombings on Boylston Street occurred. My thoughts scattered to those I knew at the finish (officials, guests, volunteers, media), those I knew in the race (at the finish and still on the course), spectators and victims I did not know and GBTC athletes I knew were running. I kept staring at the TV in the hopes of seeing people I knew. Fortunately—and it took a couple of days—I found out they were safe. The ensuing weeks here were a daze. And I had to continue with a few more interviews, which at the time seemed insignificant. But then, one after another of the interviewees told me that it was nice to talk about their memories of running in a time of no violence, even if just to separate themselves from the tragedy at hand. And then I knew: it is in this process—the continuation of running and races and community—that we will overcome such a tragedy.

Chapter One

1973–1979

The humble creation of the Greater Boston Track Club (GBTC) can be traced to 1899 England, when school presidents of turn-of-the-century Oxford and Cambridge sent word to Harvard and Yale for the four universities to compete in an exclusive U.K.-U.S. track meet. Acceptance by the Harvard-Yale team that year resulted in a 5–4 defeat of the Americans on foreign soil. But what began as a sporadically held competition soon grew to a biennial outdoor contest that alternated between countries.

In June 1973, at the twenty-fourth edition of the event, Harvard-Yale and Oxford-Cambridge battled in driving wind and rain at Harvard. So torrential was the storm that none of the one hundred meters was run above water, the cinder dirt track was a mud bath and field events were forced indoors. Behind top scores by Harvard, the U.S. schools dominated, 11–5. Ever the competitors, and since they had already planned on staying the week, Oxford-Cambridge inquired about the possibility of another meet prior to their departure. This was a tall order on such short notice, but with Boston a strong track town, it was not impossible.

When the phone rang at Boston College (BC), which housed one of only two outdoor Tartan polyurethane tracks in the nation, Jack McDonald was dispatched. An accomplished runner working in the gymnasium while finishing up his final course, he was given only days to create an international meet. Securing the facility was easy, but the collecting of race officials and athletes to support a full slate of events was not. "I needed enough for the 100, 200, 400, 800, mile, 3-mile, both sets of hurdles, high jump (HJ), long jump (LJ), triple jump (TJ), javelin, hammer, discus and shot put (SP)," he recalled.

The unofficial exhibition was successful—and dry—under the BC lights. While events were scored, there were no awards, medals or ceremony. But there was a celebration. At the time, Jack McDonald shared a five-bedroom apartment in nearby Allston, and he invited the foreign and domestic athletes over for suds and stories. This was a normal ritual for Boston-based runners anyway, albeit usually at bars such as the runners' shrine, Eliot Lounge in Boston. "It was a fun time. No trouble. You know, sometimes the most spontaneous events are the best ones," he acknowledged. "So I go back to work cleaning lockers at BC on Monday, and the compliments started coming in."

Rising from the euphoria, the idea of forming a track club began to emerge. There were some local clubs in the area, but as Jack McDonald recalled, there was really nowhere to turn for recently graduated short-distance runners who were not interested in distance events. "That's why we did it, because the other clubs were totally distance. The distance guys would do the mile and two-mile or the 10K. But there were no hurdles, no high jump—none of that stuff," he says. "That's why we started the Greater Boston Track Club, because we wanted track and field."

He began to spread the word and gather together a handful of regulars to seriously discuss it. The running community was a large but close-knit group. "In the winter, we all hung around Harvard because that was the only indoor track, and people would sneak in," he recalled. "We'd run from BC over to Harvard just to see who's around, and sometimes you'd get thrown out. And sometimes we'd bump into the guys at BoState [Boston State College]. In the springtime, because BC had the only all-weather track, everybody came to BC."

GBTC winged-foot logo first seen in March 1980. *Courtesy GBTC.*

Bill Squires in 1975. *Courtesy Jack McDonald.*

But unlike some of the few, though well-established, track clubs in the country at the time, which featured an array of All-Americans and Olympians, this potential new club would most likely be composed of a handful of blue collar–type athletes and coaches. "We just had a wonderful event, and everybody's still buzzing a little bit," Jack McDonald noted. "One thing led to another…we were all still competing, and none of us knew what we were going to do. And I called a meeting together. We probably got together to have a run or a beer or both."

Inside a locker room at BC's Roberts Center gymnasium on Thursday, August 16, 1973, Jack McDonald—by general consensus of accounts and recollections—assembled Charlie Diehl, Dave Elliott, Dick Mahoney, Kirk Pfrangle, Don Ricciato, Bob Sevene, track official Chris Lane and three coaches, John Pistone of Tufts, William "Billy" Smith of Boston University (BU) and Bill Squires of Boston State College (who in a 1980 club newsletter erroneously listed August 17, but he eventually clarified the date). And there was no waiting. Practice number one was held the following Tuesday, August 21.

"I love organizing things, and the line I like to use is: 'Don't be afraid to start small.' So we started small," said Jack McDonald. Added Sevene,

"Jack was the driving force on getting us all together and starting the club. Dick Mahoney, Bill Rodgers, Vin Fleming, Alan Milld, Jack McDonald, Don Ricciato and I were meeting on Tuesday evenings and one evening later in the week at Boston College after Jack graduated. Thus the pieces were in place." Pfrangle noted, "I distinctly recall the esprit de corps, the camaraderie, that existed. We had access to facilities, a one-of-a kind coach, an idiot savant to guide us, the synergy of the group and the excitement and enthusiasm of the first days of the running boom. It was the perfect blend of ingredients at just the right time. How could we not be successful?"

Lane, with the Massachusetts Track and Field Officials Association, commented on the inauspicious start: "Organized? Not really. A great idea? Yes, but thrown out there and developed 'on the run' most definitely. But that was also the trademark of many of those who started the GBTC."

Squires was already recognized by the National Coaches Association as Coach of the Year. "That night," said Dick Mahoney, "he walked up to us and said, 'I will coach you guys if you want.' He didn't know where we were going or what we were going to do. He didn't know if we were going to be any good or not. I give the guy a helluva lot of credit." Jack McDonald recalled, "We knew Bill Squires as a very, very good coach of kids who didn't get the scholarships to BC or BU or Northeastern. But Boston State wasn't part of the club, meaning the Greater Boston schools of the GBCs," he said in reference to the series of cross-country and track meets called the Greater Boston Championships between BC, BU, Brandeis, Harvard, MIT, Northeastern University (NU) and Tufts. "We always wished they were. They had some really good kids. As a young guy, I had a respect for the school, a respect for Coach."

In fact, if it wasn't for a scholarship to BC, Jack McDonald had planned on running for Squires. "I was going to go to Boston State because as the oldest of eleven children, my dad died when I was a freshman in high school—we were broke. We used to get stuff from Globe Santa," he said, meaning the *Boston Globe*'s charitable program created in 1956 that through donations delivers Christmas presents to families in need. "I remember going to my grandmother's house in Dorchester and in walks a box of toys from Globe Santa."

What primarily led Squires to be the head coach of GBTC was his show of faith in that group of men who thought enough of themselves and the sport to sit down and commit to forming a new track club. His own respect and love for the sport drove him to show up to that first meeting and to listen, guide and continue attending. "What I took away from my time with Coach was the selflessness," said Pfrangle. "It wasn't about being famous, cashing in on the success of the club collectively and individually, but giving back to the sport that he loved."

Additionally, one of Squires's greatest strengths was his ability to assess talent and turn just-above-average athletes into top-tier point-getters. As a coach of championship teams, the local forty-year-old was the perfect leader for this club. He was already familiar with most of the guys and their skill levels, so all he needed was to formulate a training program to match their goals. "I can train them above their ability effort," he said. "I always had them [competing] with [athletes] above their ability effort."

Ricciato recognized that importance, saying, "When Bill Squires agreed to become the official coach of the GBTC, it formalized the club into a highly competitive track and field and road-racing club." Noted Sevene, "Bill Squires helped create structure and set goals for the group as a whole. The dynamic of a group with the same goals, motivation and desire for excellence created great chemistry."

Several issues were discussed at those first meetings. One of the most important, while not necessarily the first one broached, was a name. Several were proposed, including Boston-flavored monikers such as the Beanies and the Codfishers as well as Squires's own personal favorite, the Poverty Athletic Club. Finally, it was settled on the Greater Boston Track Club, as Jack McDonald pointed out, as a connection to the GBCs, which was "the Beanpot to track and field," he noted of the famous BC-BU-Harvard-NU ice hockey tournament played annually since 1952 over two consecutive Mondays in February. He went on: "It was great. When I was coaching [track at BC], I loved it. I put a shirt and tie on. I got dressed up. The GBCs were probably the spirit, the catalyst, behind [GBTC]. We wanted to maintain that. We were alumni of it at the time, and we needed a place to train and wanted to sort of have that linkage to those colleges. We ended up training at Tufts indoors, Harvard indoors and BC outdoors. By calling us the Greater Boston Track Club, coaches and athletic directors had a sense of that."

Organization was essential, of course, and that included the naming of officers, which involved Jack McDonald as its first president and managing director, Ricciato as secretary, Squires as head coach and Pistone and Billy Smith as assistant coaches. Around this time, Jack McDonald had also procured a job as a social director of a suburban apartment complex,

Amateur Athletic Union (AAU) Team Championship patch. *Courtesy Jack McDonald.*

where he would clean the pool, the bathrooms and play cribbage with the residents. That soon became one of the unofficial club headquarters, where several times a year they would meet at the function room to socialize and relax. There was also an old typewriter there that was used for the early club newsletters.

Topics of funds, training schedules, and competitions also arose early on. "[Because of] all our experiences in the collegiate world, we knew the schedule and what we could get into," explained Jack McDonald. "There were things like Squires's Codfish [Bowl Cross-Country] Invitational [and] Boston State Invitational that he allowed us to run in; the New England AAU [Amateur Athletic Union] championships in the 15K, 20K [and] cross-country; and in track and field, there were meets in armories."

Squires formulated his training based on the talent he had. He mixed roadwork and track work in a cocktail of sessions that combined speed, distance, endurance, hills and fun. Part of those workouts included the most difficult section of the Boston Marathon course—Heartbreak Hill, the notorious fourth Newton hill located near the twenty-one-mile mark adjacent to BC.

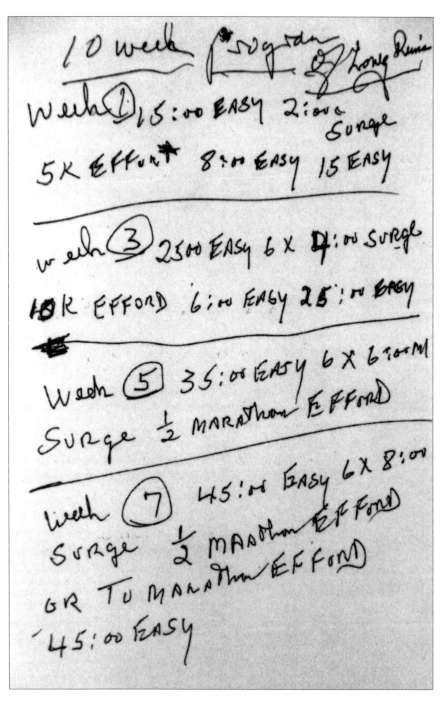

Scribbled workout from Bill Squires. *Courtesy Mark Duggan.*

"My favorite workout with Bill Squires is what he referred to as a simulator. We ran this workout in the fall to prepare for racing five miles at Franklin Park," said Sevene of the oft-used championship locale. As for the workout, he detailed it as follows: "[Run a] mile on the old outdoor track at Boston College at 4:35 [pace], proceed out the gate at about 75 percent effort and run over to Heartbreak Hill; two hill repeats, 90 percent effort to bench on top—700 yards—of Heartbreak Hill. After second hill repeat, back to Boston College at 75 percent effort, enter track through gate and directly run two miles on the track. Average around 4:45 pace. No stopping throughout the whole workout. [That] workout was a great way for preparing for racing at Franklin Park."

Ricciato, who also favored simulators, noted, "During cross-country season, we would start from the track at BC, run a four-mile loop on the roads at a brisk pace. Immediately upon completing the four-mile, run back to the track. We would start a mile on the track at 4:40 pace. Coach believed that this replicated the fatigue and oxygen debt you would experience in a race. During track season, Coach had us run three to four repeats [of] three-quarters of a mile at about 3:05 to 3:10 pace. At the end of the three-quarters-of-a-mile run, we would immediately jog for about ten seconds and run a quarter mile as fast as we could. This again was meant to 'simulate' the fatigue in a race."

GBTC was also a club without a house. While it had no facility, no home track and no operational base, it did possess a great amount of ingenuity and resourcefulness. It was not uncommon for its athletes to jump the fence at BC to gain access to the Eagles' track. Fortunately, Squires was friends with the athletic director, who repeatedly requested that the coach notify him ahead of time so he could unlock the gate.

The first competition as a club—a mere ten weeks after that initial meeting—was the 1973 National AAU 20K Championships, which it won (the first of nine straight). Sevene recalled, "I was no distance runner, per say, but training with Billy (Rodgers), Hodgie (Bob Hodge), Vinnie and Dickie Mahoney during the summer and fall, I got recruited to run the race. I was in the lead pack when we went through Cape Ann and it dawned on me that I better back off if I was not going to die a slow death. I finished twelfth, and we won the national title; but that was the race where we had to run through a fire on our way back through Gloucester."

With a limited number of runners with whom to work, Squires decided to primarily focus on the relay. In its first indoor track season (1973–74), GBTC competed in the 1973 BC Relays, thanks in part to the generous invitation

GBTC 4 x 800 relay team at the Millrose Games. *From left*: Don Ricciato, Dave Elliot, Bob Sevene and Jack McDonald. *Manning Solon photo courtesy Bob Sevene.*

from Eagle coach Bill Gilligan. The two-mile relay team (Ricciato, Sevene, Elliott and Jack McDonald) immediately began to place, with top-three showings at the New York Knights of Columbus (first), Olympic Invitational (second) and National AAU (third).

Regarding the early success, Jack McDonald confessed, "It was pretty satisfying but also not surprising, because we knew what we had as a group and we knew what was out there. We did have quick success, but we should have. Selfishly, as far as myself and the three of us [in the relay], this was why we started the track club, so that we could have a home and a place to train in the events that we knew the best. That was fulfilling our dream. But at the same token, we had to have some financial backing to have some social fun, to have a track if we wanted our two-mile relay; so we made sure we needed to provide competition and training sites for the other events—the hurdlers, the shot-putters."

While the foursome rarely practiced handoffs, they did endure a fair amount of speedwork. Jack McDonald and Sevene were predominantly milers and Elliott and Ricciato half-milers, so there were times when their workouts differed. But the constant was speed. "When we were 'on the watch,' as I used to say with Coach, it was a lot of speedwork—200s, 300s, 400s, every once in a while 600s," Jack McDonald recalled. "While they [Elliott and Ricciato] might run 400s, I would run 600s because I would be getting ready for a big mile later in the year. But basically, we worked together all the time."

However, Jack McDonald did recall one 4 x 400 in particular when, due to a snowstorm, one of the relay members failed to show. No one in the 4 x 800 wanted to fill in because that relay was later in the meet, so after some discussion and since they never won the 4 x 400 anyway, "we figured we're paying our own money, we trained hard—we've gotta run. It's Madison Square Garden, the place was filled up with 18,000 people. Just run three," he says. "So, I think it was Mark Young, Jim O'Brien and Leo Dunn. Mark, who ran with Frank Shorter at Yale, led off and was in first place. Jimmy, second leg—and once you get the lead on these board tracks it's a major advantage because everybody behind you sort of gets slowed—was in first place. And Leo kept it going. I was with Squires and he's going, 'Oh, God!' All of a sudden we're in first place. [And when] the third man went to hand to the fourth man and there's no fourth man, and we stepped off the track, you could hear this murmur from 18,000 people. And Squires said, 'We're never going to be invited back to this meet again,'" he laughed (GBTC did return). To punctuate the feat, Fred Doyle—GBTC's 4:05:04 miler—chortled, "They won the three-legged relay in Millrose!"

Around the fall of 1973, Bill Rodgers entered the picture. At the time, he was competing for the Boston Athletic Association (BAA) under John "Jock" Semple, the animated Scottish trainer who was also the public face of the Boston Marathon and a good friend of Squires (who had been a BAA member since the 1950s). The twenty-five-year-old 1970 Wesleyan track and cross-country Cardinal—whose collegiate teammates had included his roommate, 1968 Boston Marathon winner Ambrose "Amby" Burfoot, and 1972 U.S. Olympian Jeff Galloway—was growing increasingly interested in long-distance running, especially the marathon. With a voracious appetite for all things running, Rodgers, while not all that familiar with the newborn club, was to some extent aware of its members.

Squires recalled that the first time he heard of Rodgers was in the late 1960s in a running magazine preview story on schools to watch in the New England cross-country championships. "I knew Amby and Galloway," he said. "I read *Track & Field News* and everything. Rodgers wasn't known as much as Galloway—and Amby won Boston as a sophomore—but I knew

Bill Squires (left) and Bill Rodgers. *Photo by Paul C. Clerici.*

him. Imagine having Rodgers, Galloway and Amby? Are you kidding me? On a distance medley, on a four-mile relay, in cross-country?"

The first time the coach remembered seeing Rodgers in person was at a competition where Squires was with his athletes. Squires described their first encounter: "He walks over, and he has friggin' rag-clothes on. He had a ponytail, but I had read about him. I said, 'Oh, you're BAA. Can I help you?' And he said, 'Oh, yeah. I'd like you to help me.' I told him I knew he was a serious runner, so he could come down and run with us. He said, 'You don't mind me working with you?' I said no, but I told him he's not going to try to join my club because he's running for the BAA, and I am still running for the BAA. And Jock is a very fine man." Rodgers suggested he could join the GBTC in December, even though by changing club affiliations, he would be forced to run unattached for several months before officially competing for another club. He was not deterred. Rodgers had already had his first attempt at the Boston

Marathon in April 1973 but had dropped out near BC. Later that year, he ran the Bay State Marathon.

Tom Derderian, who joined GBTC in 1978 but ran the 1973 Bay State with Rodgers, recalled, "He said that he had never finished a marathon before; so I said just run with me, and we'll get through and you can finish. So we ran the first five miles, chatting in about fiftieth place, and we went a little faster the next five-mile loop, and then a little faster. And with five miles to go, Billy said he felt pretty good and wanted to pick it up. I picked it up to 5:20s, and he picked it up to 5-minute miles and he wound up winning the race." Rodgers's time was a course record (CR), 2:28:12.

In late 1973, Rodgers did leave the BAA for GBTC. "I liked the team aspect of GBTC," he said. Squires, for his part, smoothed things over with Semple in case there was any potential animosity from the fiery Scot. But all was forgiven when Squires reassured Semple that he had, in fact, advised Rodgers to stay with the BAA. "I did," Squires said, "I swore I did. I didn't want people to think I was stealing guys from other clubs." Semple believed him, and they remained friends.

The claim to fame thus far for the club was the relay. Sevene recalled one meet in particular that still resonates. At the 1974 National AAU, the two-mile relay went up against, among others, a University of Chicago Track Club (UCTC) that featured Notre Dame All-American and U.S. Olympian Rick Wohlhuter. "It was the first year of the GBTC's existence, and Bill Squires had taken a ragtag group of middle-distance guys," he said. "Rick was running the third leg [for UCTC] because he had just won the 1,000-yard run thirty minutes prior. I was running the third leg [for GBTC] and was sitting on [Rick], and I realized with two laps to go—it was a 160-yard track—that Bill was [standing] in lane two, screaming for me to blow past him, which I did." After UCTC won, "I remember Rick asking me who the crazy guy was on the track and me telling him [it was Squires and that] he was a very good runner at Notre Dame in his day. And he laughed like crazy. Two things I personally remember about that race: one, how proud Billy was and how good it made me feel; and two, Dave Elliott digging down and running beyond belief."

GBTC's relay success continued into the 1974 outdoors when it was third in the distance medley relay (DMR)—a race with varying legs of 1,200, 400, 800 and 1,600 meters—at the fabled Penn Relays, third in the two-mile relay at the National AAU and won the NEAAU (New England Amateur Athletic Union). GBTC also won the National AAU 20K and the New England championships. And Rodgers chalked up more individual successes with a

Bob Sevene running his leg of the 4 x 800 relay at the Olympic Invitational. *Courtesy Bob Sevene.*

2:19:34, placing fourteenth, at the 1974 Boston Marathon, as well as wins at the NEAAU six-miler, Greater Boston International six-miler and 1974 Falmouth Road Race in a CR of 34:16. The Squires training was paying off for everyone.

"The most difficult workout the first year was the beginning of outdoor track [training] at Boston College," said Sevene. "Jack, Don, Dave and I were doing twelve 400s on Boston College's outdoor track in early April in a rain-, sleet-, snowstorm. Our hands were so cold after the workout that we could not take off our spikes. We had to walk to Roberts Center in spikes, where Coach Billy Smith had to remove the spikes because my fingers did not function." Pfrangle points to the various BC loops and Sunday long runs as pivotal to his success, saying, "I have always felt that those runs toughened me up mentally as well as physically. The Sunday morning runs would start out fairly easily—lots of good talk and back-and-forth banter—but they, too, would eventually become races. They were exhausting, but invaluable to my development. Relative to the others, I was still at the back, but I knew that I was improving all the time. Nothing breeds success like success." While it did occasionally occur, workout racing was discouraged. "Oh, yeah," said Dick Mahoney. "If someone got carried away and ran fast, we'd get mad at him and guys'd start yelling. Coach taught us that. He'd say there's a time to race, a time to train. Rodgers was good at that, too."

Derderian concurred. In reference to workouts when he joined in 1978, he said: "You had a bunch of animals who were quite capable of tearing each other apart. But the workouts were controlled by all of these guys who did not want to make every single interval into a race. When we said we were going to run a mile in five minutes, we ran a mile in five minutes. You were not there to win the workout. That's what races are for. When someone was showing off at a workout and winning the intervals, Squires would pick up a piece of trash from Burger King blowing in the wind and fashion a hat out of it—a crown—and crown that guy King of the Workout [an unwanted honor]. When it was your turn in a workout to lead, you led in the time prescribed. And the long intervals that we did in groups made the races seem like practice."

The team's successes began to get noticed and, as a result, attracted new members. Bob Hodge, a teammate of Fleming's from Johnson & Wales Junior College, was one. "In 1974, I spotted the results of the second Falmouth Road Race in the newspaper," Hodge recalled. "GBTC dominated, and Rodgers won over Marty Liquori (of Villanova). I was not running much at the time, but seeing this, it motivated me to contact Vin, and I started heading to Boston—Jamaica Plain—on weekends to run with Vin and Rodgers and others. Through him, I became a member of GBTC." It was "mostly the group dynamic, the workouts at Boston College and the socializing at the Eliot Lounge" that appealed to Hodge.

In its second cross-country season, the GBTC achieved several wins: the 1974 NU Cross-Country five-miler with the first three spots, which included Rodgers's victorious 24:18; the New England 15K Championship, with Rodgers's CR of 46:28 on a suspected short course; the NEAAU championships, with Rodgers in first at 29:18; and the National AAU 20K title (for the second time), with Rodgers in second, Scott Graham in eleventh, Fleming in fourteenth, Joe Crowley in eighteenth and a surprised Jack McDonald, who admittedly loathed distance runs, in twenty-third. But when Jack McDonald had earned points at the previous week's 15K with a fifth place, Squires had taken notice. "Yeah, I actually ran pretty good, and I hated every second of it," he said with a laugh. "I had agreed to run the 15K, but I was not doing the friggin' 20K! And Squires calls me the following

Tuesday because somebody got hurt, I think, so I knew what he wanted when he called. But he brainwashed me into thinking it would be good for my mile if I ran the 20K. And how do you say no to Coach?"

Also in 1974, in a peek into the future, at the Massachusetts State High School Cross-Country Championship 2.5-mile race, the top two finishers were Dan Dillon of Chicopee Comprehensive High School (first, CR 14:02) and Alberto Salazar of Wayland High School (second, 14:05). In a remarkable twist of fate, both schoolboy harriers would soon become part of the GBTC legacy, in addition to that of Providence College (PC) and the University of Oregon, respectively.

The club benefited from Squires's skill as a multilayered

Dan Dillon, who ran for GBTC, and his wife, Patti (Lyons) (Catalano) Dillon, who ran for the BAA. *Photo by Paul C. Clerici.*

leader. He simultaneously coached his GBTC athletes as a team and as individuals, in that there were team titles for which to compete and individuals who competed for their own wins. And his tutelage paid off again in 1975. The two-mile relay team (Ricciato, Sevene, Elliott and Jack McDonald) won the Olympic Invitational and was fourth at the National AAU. GBTC won its second consecutive New England indoors and, in outdoors, won the National AAU 30K, National AAU 20K and New Englands and came in third at the National AAU relay championships.

"I thought that it was clear that the club was going places based on, initially, the success of the two-mile relay as we competed at some of the major indoor competitions," Ricciato pointed out. He went into more detail: "Shortly after the success of the two-mile relay, the club was attracting some of the best post-collegiate runners in the New England area. BC became a weekly meeting place for distance training on the roads and track workouts. Each week at BC, it became a mecca for runners looking to continue competitive running after college. The combination of cross-country and road-racing training in the fall, followed by training on the track in the winter and spring, led to a high level of fitness. This resulted in many on the team running PRs at a range of events. Squires's challenging workouts had everyone ready to perform at an optimal level."

And Rodgers continued to shine. By 1975, he had already been in five marathons, including a DNF (did not finish) at the 1973 Boston, and had achieved two wins (1973 Bay State, 1974 Philadelphia), a fifth place (1974 New York), a fourteenth place (1974 Boston) and two CRs (Bay State, Philadelphia). And he was still hungry, especially for Boston.

To win the Boston Marathon, Squires knew what was needed. Rodgers, at twenty-seven, was improving. And Squires—who at twenty-eight had been twentieth at the 1961 Boston (2:47:46)—understood the commitment required and the steps involved. "I'm trying to divide the first half of the course, the middle part of the course and then the end part where he'd gut his way," Squires planned. "And with about three weeks to go, I would tailor the workouts. You see, they would go into your brain, and you'd understand what it is, that that's the way the race was going to go."

Rodgers was fourth at the 1975 U.S. Men's Cross-Country 12,000-Meter Trials. With repeated club and individual success, some of the media began to pick up on Rodgers, so Squires, in an attempt to diffuse and absorb any extra attention, let "slip" that "Will Rogers" was running well. Later, in the *Boston Globe*, there was the reference to a Will Rogers of Jamaica Plain. "Geez, they bought it," Squires says with a hearty laugh. "Will Rogers! See, they thought I knew everything, so they printed it."

On a more serious note, Squires targeted for Rodgers the prestigious IAAF (International Association of Athletics Federations) World Cross-Country Championship 12K in Morocco on March 16 as not only a fine tuneup for Boston but also a feather in the cap for Americans. Recalled Rodgers of the race, "What happened was it was just a burst of adrenaline because I forgot my racing shoes. I borrowed a pair of spikes from Gary Tuttle (of Humboldt State University)—he made the team—and they fit like a glove. The gun went off, I moved up into the lead, and the next thing I knew, I was racing for the lead. I was going for it. When you get into the lead, and if you can, you duke it out. That was it the whole way. We broke away. When it came time for the kick, Ian Stewart took off, and Mariano Haro went with him. And I tried to go with him." In a remarkable 35:27.4, Rodgers won bronze. "I was high as a kite! I ran seven miles after the race. I was wired."

Bill Rodgers wore these running shoes from Steve Prefontaine and this hand-lettered shirt when he won the 1975 Boston Marathon. *Running Past photo by Andy Yelenak.*

While it was truly a rare and major international achievement, Squires hoped the local media would not pounce on it too much and put a spotlight on Rodgers for Boston. But those in the running community knew the significance. Three weeks later, 1972 U.S. Olympian and legendary multiple record–holder Steve "Pre" Prefontaine, who was working for a fledgling running shoe company in Oregon, wrote Rodgers a letter and mailed him some new running shoes. On April 21, at the seventy-ninth Boston Marathon, in an American record (AR) and CR of 2:09:55 and in those very running shoes from Pre (who tragically died in a car accident thirty-nine days later), Rodgers was victorious. One of GBTC's very own runners could now say, "In 1975, I won Boston in a pair of Nike Boston racing shoes given to me by Steve Prefontaine just a few weeks earlier." And regarding the prized footwear, Rodgers noted, "The shoes were light and flexible. When [afterward,] the *Boston Globe* photographer took a photo of the balls of my feet—in a podiatrist's search for blisters—there were none. The shoes were perfect."

It was a triumph for Rodgers and the club, especially because hand-drawn across the front of his shirt was the word BOSTON and the initials GBTC for all to see throughout the entire race (and accompanying media coverage). None of the parties involved—the runner, the club and Squires—would ever be the same.

"[Regarding] my racing singlet from 1975, I recall having found it in a trash bin on a run," says Rodgers. "My wife at the time, Ellen, wrote BOSTON with GBTC in big letters underneath with Magic Marker dark ink so folks could see I was a local boy and might cheer for me." And cheer they did.

Rodgers reflected on his Boston win: "Jock Semple and Coach knew I was ready to race for the win as I'd just taken the bronze at the World Cross-Country Championships in Rabat, Morocco. That world cross-country medal and my 1975 Boston medal mean a lot to me, as it took three years of marathon training with my GBTC teammates—Bob Hodge, Vin Fleming, Randy Thomas, Bob Sevene, Fred Doyle, Mark Duggan, Walter Murphy, Dick Mahoney, Alberto Salazar, Don Ricciato and many others—to get these medals. To this day, only four American men [Tracy Smith, Rodgers, Craig Virgin and Salazar] have medaled in the Senior Men's World Cross-Country. Alberto and I—two GBTC racers—make up half of them. I know Alberto thanks Coach Squires for his support and guidance, and so do I."

That group training also resulted in a third-place team finish at the 1975 Boston Marathon with Rodgers, Graham and Fleming. In addition, major wheelchair history was made when teammate Bob Hall finished in 2:58:00 as the lone competitor, thus forever securing a place in the Boston Marathon for wheelchair athletes. "It was exhilarating, felt like a training mile," Bob Hall said of the milestone and added about some of the sights

At a 1976 road race in Quincy, Fred Doyle (64), Bill Rodgers (180) and Mark Duggan (195).
Courtesy Fred Doyle.

and sounds: "People on trees, signs and telephone poles and literally a great deal of horseshit from police horses [securing the course then], and the smell of sausages."

It was at Boston State College where student-athlete Bob Hall had first approached Professor Squires. "Bill was one of my health and physical education teachers," he said. "Many of my classmates belonged [to GBTC]. He was trying to help those who wanted to continue after college. It was a natural to go to him about racing the mile at weekly track meets." Squires put Bob Hall through the same kind of hard training, albeit altered for wheels, especially in relation to banking on the track. "We all had different workouts based on fitness level and distance; trying to achieve [your] best performance," noted Bob Hall. "Bill Rodgers and I enjoyed the camaraderie on and off the track, especially participating in races and the Eliot Lounge. [At GBTC] we were all one and equal."

Bob Hall then wanted to increase his mileage and race distance, to the point where he earned multiple distance national honors. "The day before

Seated, from left: Bill Rodgers and Bob Hall, being interviewed as fellow GBTC alum and Boston Marathon race director Dave McGillivray (background) chats with U.S. Olympic Marathon gold medalist Joan Benoit Samuelson. *Photo by Paul C. Clerici.*

leaving for the National Wheelchair Mile in 1974, Coach Squires and I passed each other in the hallway of Boston State," he recalled. "I told him I was ready, and he turned to me and said, while pointing a finger, 'Hey, I sent two guys to the nationals and the third is coming back a champion!' I did! And I also won the first National Wheelchair Marathon within two months in 1974."

All of this continued notoriety at the club attracted more attention and more athletes. As Sevene recalled of that 1975 Boston Marathon, "This one race brought the GBTC, Bill Rodgers and Bill Squires into the

**AMATEUR
ATHLETIC
UNION OF THE UNITED STATES, INC**

58 District Associations Servin
Amateur Athletics in *Twenty* Spor
A.A.U. HOUS

INDIANAPOLIS, INDIANA 462

Cable Address: "AMATHLETIC" Indianapol

NATIONAL OFFICER
President, DAVID G. RIVENE

First Vice President, JOSEPH R. SCALZ

Second Vice President, JOEL FERREI

Secretary, RICHARD E. HARKIN

Treasurer, CLARENCE JOHNSO

September 5, 1974

Mr. Jack McDonald
Greater Boston Track Club

Braintree, Mass.   02184

Dear Jack:

Thank you very much for your recent letter concerning
club aid. We have not been able to help clubs this past
year, and do not anticipate any opportunity to do so in
the near future.

Thank you very much for your inquiry and best of luck to
you as well as your club.

Very truly yours,

Robert C. Lafferty
Track and Field Administrator

RCL/rr

cc: Ollan C. Cassell
     Col. Jesse R. Liscomb

AAU fund request rejection letter that GBTC received in 1974. *Courtesy Jack McDonald.*

Gurnet Classic Beach Run logo. *Courtesy Jack McDonald.*

national spotlight." And Bob Hall, too, whose 2:40:18 at the 1977 Boston was a world best time.

With funding still a concern, Jack McDonald held meetings to discuss the treasury's zero balance. He had even written the AAU for club aid but received a rejection letter from the track and field administrator.

So they turned to what they knew best: running. In August 1975, the first fundraising six-mile Gurnet Classic Beach Run was held. The brainchild of Jack McDonald, the race's inaugural field was populated by about 120 people. One of the quirks was the start time, which fluctuated due to the course's unique location on a narrow strip of beachfront heavily affected by the tide. "There's a fish market near there, and I'd go down New Year's Day and get the tide chart; and that's when I'd pick the time," explains Jack McDonald, whose responsibilities were later taken on by Steve Calder and Sharpless Jones. "People would never know when the Gurnet Classic would be because we had to go when the tide was low on a Saturday afternoon. It was a lot of fun. It was a giant happy hour."

Added Dick Mahoney about the footing, "Oh, it was horrible." He laughed, "At the start, the beach was very nice. But the farther out you got, the footing got softer and uneven. And I remember when Jack was giving out the medals [to GBTCers], he'd hand you the medal and tell you [in a whisper] to hand it back because he didn't have enough." That first year, Gurnet was reportedly "won" by Salazar, Rodgers and Mark Duggan in 32:48 (yes, a three-way tie), followed by Fleming and Hodge in 33:47 (yes, a two-way tie). At any rate, some of the GBTC and non-GBTC running greats who competed over the years who were cheered on by hundreds of

From left: Alberto Salazar, Mark Duggan and Bill Rodgers in the Gurnet Classic. *Courtesy Jack McDonald.*

spectators lining the beaches, included the likes of John Gregorek, Dick Mahoney, Kevin Ryan, Steve Scott and Randy Thomas.

Big-name runners were now beginning to race in the Bay State. The Falmouth Road Race, created by marquee Eliot barkeep Tommy Leonard and which predated GBTC in 1973 by one day, featured a stellar lineup of talent, including many GBTC runners. "Bill Squires brought down all the horses. They gave us some dignity, some class," Leonard credited. "They knew how to have a good time, but they never got out of line at the Eliot. They were just a great band of brothers. They were a dream clientele. They were gentlemen—I remember that distinctly."

Early Falmouth elite battles between GBTC and non-GBTC runners included several epic match-ups:

1974: Rodgers (first), Villanova's Liquori (second).

1975: Florida Track Club's Shorter (first), Rodgers (second). The race was billed as Shorter-Rodgers I.

1976: Shorter (first), Rodgers (second)—Shorter-Rodgers II.

1977: Rodgers (first), Salazar (second).

Tommy Leonard with the plaque honoring him at the Falmouth Road Race start line. *Photo by Paul C. Clerici.*

1978: Rodgers (first), Mike Roche (second). This year the field included nearly ten Olympians, a dozen sub-4:00 milers, sixteen national champions, including teammates Rodgers, Roche, Bruce Bickford (seventh), Hodge (eighth), Greg Meyer (ninth), Salazar (tenth).

1979: St. Louis Track Club's Virgin (first), Rodgers (third).

"It's sort of fun," said Meyer of competing against his buddies. "I'm friends with all of them. But Billy knows, when the gun goes off, you race each other; when the race is done, you go back to being friends. I mean, he's tough!"

An example of this occurred when Rodgers clandestinely hydrated at the start of the oppressive 1978 Falmouth Road Race. He skipped water in the early miles, which prompted Salazar—unaware of Rodgers's prior water intake—to stay with Rodgers, also skip water and push himself to near death. By the time he reached the baking beachfront finish, Salazar's body temperature reportedly rose to 108 degrees, and he was given last rites.

Funds from Gurnet weren't enough, however. That's where the inventive frugalness of Squires came into play. While traveling to away meets or out-of-state competitions, the norm at hotels was to have only a few team members check in and the rest pile in the room, separate the bed into its mattress and box spring and decide who sleeps where, as Squires often secured the bathtub as his bed. "That's a true story—or on the floor—and sometimes, he would use the shower curtain as his blanket because he wanted us to sleep in a bed. We'd all stuff ourselves in a room—five, six, seven of us," Jack McDonald said with a laugh. "And we'd jump at the chance to do it again."

The 1975 cross-country season was filled with many highlights. GBTC won the New England 15K with Hodge first (CR 45:29), Thomas second, Charlie Duggan fourth, Doyle tenth and Art Dulong twelfth; the National AAU 20K with Rodgers second, Hodge sixth, Thomas seventh, Dulong nineteenth and Dick Mahoney twenty-fourth; the NEAAU with Hodge second, Dulong third, Graham fourth, Rick Neckas eighth and Doyle ninth; and the NU Invitational. Rodgers and Hodge took first and second at the Lowell Half-Marathon. And with his third-place 2:11:26 at Japan's 1975 Fukuoka International Open Marathon Championship, Rodgers was ranked number one in the United States and the world by *Track & Field News*, the first such major recognition for GBTC.

At the 1975 Massachusetts State High School Cross-Country Championship 2.5-miler, Salazar improved on his second-place showing the previous year with a 14:11 win. Two weeks later, at the 1975 National AAU 10,000, for GBTC the sixteen-year-old was twenty-fourth (29:39) in front of Thomas, Mark Duggan, Hodge and Graham. The Rookie, as he was called, was steadily bursting onto the scene. "Kirk brought me to the GBTC workouts twice per week—in the winter to Tufts and in the spring and summer to BC—and I got to run with a lot of guys that were better than me, and they taught me a lot," Salazar noted. "They were very friendly and took me under their wings, so I felt welcomed by the runners and by Coach Squires. He put me in a group that I was ready to run with on any particular day, but by the second year, I was running the same workout as the top runners. He would give me workouts to do on my own, back in Wayland, as well, so they were customized for me as well when necessary," said Salazar, who added that among his highlights was "just overall to be traveling with guys that were a lot of fun, more than the race themselves."

GBTC continued to earn respect and accolades on the track. Jack McDonald peaked in 1976, when, at the Dartmouth Relays, he put together the best mile of his life. While he never set out to run a four-minute mile, that threshold was always present: "I can never say it was a goal, but when you're a miler, it's there. There were the ten-second 100, the four-minute

Alberto Salazar (left) and Bill Rodgers at Boston College, circa 1975. *Courtesy Bob Sevene.*

mile and the seven-foot high jump as the magic things that we all grew up with as kids. We were living in the [sub-four-minute milers] Jim Ryun-Steve Prefontaine-Marty Liquori world, and everybody's chasing the four-minute mile and got as close as they could. But I was a runner that preferred to get a good place than a good time. I would rather win the New Englands in 4:20 than be third in 4:05."

Jack McDonald's mile-running style was to sit back and then pick it up, whereas others might charge right out of the gate. This was partly due to the fact that in a meet, he would usually run the mile and half-mile as well as the two-mile relay, so he needed to conserve some effort. While Dartmouth was utilized to qualify for the nationals the following month, it was still a top competition on its own. The week before, Squires held one of his equalizing runoffs—a 1,000-yard time trial—to determine who would compete at Dartmouth and also to prep for the 4:09 mile national's qualifying mark.

"We go through the 800 in 1:51, 1:52," recalled Jack McDonald of the 1,000. He averaged a 1:52 in the half-mile, 2:11 in the 1,000 and 4:07 in the mile. "I finish and I'm huffing and puffing, and I look over to Coach; and he's looking at his old stopwatch. He's going crazy, moving his arms around. I'm not going over to him because he doesn't look happy, that maybe I ran a bad time. Finally I go over and say, 'Coach, what's the matter? Not fast enough?' He goes, 'Not fast enough? You just ran the fastest time in the world!' He shows me his watch and it says 2:06.9, which was the fastest in the world. I was like, 'What are we gonna do?'" A timer next to Squires confirmed the result, and thinking no one would believe them, they called it in to *Track & Field News* as a 2:07.

At Dartmouth's invitational mile, Jack McDonald's goal was to run that 4:09 for the nationals. With a goal time in mind, he decided to alter his tactics and, instead of his usual sit-and-kick approach, shoot out at the gun: "I needed to get 4:09, so I went out to take it. Off I went, and I was in the lead. I did a 60[-second] for the first quarter, 1:30 for three laps, 2:00 for four laps, 3:00 at three-quarters—and I heard it. After you lead for six laps, you're starting to get either bored or tired or both. All of a sudden, Jim Peterson of Georgetown passed me, which was probably the best thing to happen to me because then the win juices kicked in. I didn't hear the split at one lap to go, which was probably 3:30. The place was going crazy! I stayed right with Jimmy and I couldn't catch him."

Peterson won in a time of 4:00.9, and Jack McDonald was second, just off his shoulder. "I was right there, but I knew that, at the time, before electric timing, when people were that close to each other it's possible to have the same time. And I wondered—it'd be nice if they gave me 4:00.9 instead of 4:01. It just sounds better. And they did, they gave me 4:00.9. That was probably a bigger joy to see than to win the race. It was like, 'Wow, the stars lined up!' I was still trying to beat the guy; the juices to win just kicked in." At the National AAU, Jack McDonald found himself at the start line literally shoulder-to-shoulder with world record-holders John Walker of New Zealand and Filbert Bayi of Tanzania. But he did not have a repeat performance. GBTC did, however, come in third in the two-mile relay.

GBTC closed out the 1975–76 indoors with several top finishes. And at the 1976 American Legion Marsh Post #442 handicap race, Pfrangle won by fully utilizing his training. "This is the highlight of my running career, the one race that I want etched on my headstone," he declared of the twelve-mile race in which runners begin in staggered starts based on pace. He continued to describe the win: "I was one of the last people to start and I chased people for twelve miles on a cool day in Cambridge. The last couple miles were along Memorial Drive, into a very strong headwind with sleet and freezing rain. It was miserable, awful, but I was in a zone. I was rolling. I caught the last runner a few hundred yards from the finish. I was exhausted, frozen, and absolutely overjoyed that I had won the race. Coach was at the finish, and to this day, he still reminds me of my performance that day every time we are together."

Overlapping the outdoor and road-race seasons—which included the (in) famous 7.6-uphill-mile Mount Washington Road Race won by Hodge in the first of his record seven wins—was the 1976 U.S. Olympic Trials. At the Trials marathon, Rodgers qualified with his second-place finish (2:11:58). A month later, he won his 10,000 qualifying heat (28:32.79), and three days afterward at the 10,000 Trials he came in fourth (28:04.42). Between the Trials and the Games, the July 5, 1976 issue of *Sports Illustrated* featured a cover story on the American track and field team—"Next Stop, Montreal"—and a cover photo from the 10,000 Trials that showed Shorter, Garry Bjorklund and Rodgers. For the young club, this was yet another first on a major scale.

In the Olympic Marathon on June 22 in Montreal, Canada, Rodgers faded to fortieth (2:25:14) due in part to a previous ankle injury. Also in 1976, Squires was named New England AAU Men's Track and Field chairman, and in cross-country the club won the National AAU 20K for the fourth consecutive year, the NU Invitational again and the NEAAU 10,000 with four in the top ten (Mark Duggan third, Thomas fourth, Doyle fifth and Dick Mahoney ninth). One big blemish was a disappointing ninth at the National AAU 10,000, a major goal of Squires's, who ached to capture this elusive crown. Rodgers, eager to erase his Olympic Marathon bitter taste, blazed a CR 2:10:09 at the 1976 New York City, his first of four straight wins there. In 1976, he was ranked third in the United States and sixth in the world by *Track & Field News*.

For the rest of the decade in cross-country and track, GBTC as a team recorded a phenomenal combined twelve top-three National AAU and U.S. placings and eight top-three New England showings, including seven National AAU titles, two U.S. Cross-Country Trial wins and four New England titles.

At four years old, the club took a few major steps into adulthood. In 1977, GBTC's Tom Grilk of the Hale and Dorr law firm incorporated the club with the commonwealth as a tax exempt 501(c)(3); a governing board of directors was instituted; and another fundraiser was created in the Freedom Trail Road Race. Located in Boston, the eight-miler was another success, whose sponsor would change many times over its ten-year run. That first year succeeded thanks to Jack McDonald (who was beginning to step away

Right: Bill Rodgers winning the 1976 New York City Marathon. *Courtesy Bob Sevene.*

Below, from left: Leo Dunn, Dan Fyre, Jack McDonald and Don Ricciato in 1976. *Courtesy Jack McDonald.*

from GBTC to start coaching at BC), Don Facey, Grilk and Todd Miller, along with initial inklings from Leonard and GBTC's Scott McAllister of Labatt Brewery Company. It was modeled after the Atlanta Track Club's Peachtree Road Race, which started in 1970. As GBTC's Fred Treseler recalled, the club's initial approach differed from other one-and-done races in that money was put back into the race.

According to Grilk, it all started in a fast-evolving meeting he attended with Leonard, McAllister and Jack McDonald. "I had written up a proposal for Labatt to sponsor the track club, but when Scott said they only sponsored events, I said we had a race. Jack said it was a Boston race, and Tommy said it was a waterfront race. All of that was made up on the spot. The course came from places that I could see either from my apartment on Beacon Street or my office on State Street, [composed] mainly of places that I thought it would be fun to run but where one was not normally able to do so. Jack and I would go out on Sunday mornings to set up the course, with Rodgers occasionally coming along. [And there was] Dave McGillivray, whom we sent over to Charlestown in my old Mustang convertible with Bob Sevene in hopes of preventing anything bad from happening as the runners went up and down Bunker Hill."

Freedom Trail Road Race. *Courtesy Fred Doyle.*

That first year, the BC marching band serenaded an amazing field that included Dillon, Fleming, Hodge, Rodgers and Thomas of GBTC; local national cross-country champion Lynn Jennings; winners of the previous three Bostons in Jack Fultz, Kim Merritt and Jerome Drayton; and 1976 U.S. Olympians Bjorklund, Don Kardong and Shorter. Grilk, Pat Lynch and John McGrath, with assistance from many others, helped the race continue.

"[We] tackled shutting down huge sections of downtown Boston for one of the first prize-money events ever staged in the road-race world at a time when the AAU and amateur status still prevailed. Pretty gutsy of us, in retrospect, but at the time, it just seemed like the thing to do," noted McGrath of the editions in the 1980s. Added Grilk about its success, "Raising money, working against the then-prevalent amateurism standards, battling with and vanquishing the AAU and, above all, establishing an event that was fun for pretty much everyone—and still one that raised money so that elite runners could run. It was the advent of John and Pat in 1978 that brought organization to it all. Pat brought marketing and soul to it; John brought process and discipline. It showed the way in road-race operation. John brought all of that into play before there was ever [race management companies], and it led to the Milk Run, the downtown Thanksgiving race, and a bunch of others that helped launch an industry."

The early coordinated efforts included several facilities with GBTC member ties: Bill Rodgers Running Center at nearby Faneuil Hall Marketplace (Rodgers); the office of Boston mayor Kevin White (Lynch); First Security Services (McGrath); Harvard Business School (Rodney Pearson); Facey Sport Printers (Facey); and Hale and Dorr (Grilk). "[In the second year] we installed our race phone service at Bill's store and ran sort of an office there," explained McGrath. He continued: "Pat handled getting the necessary permits and clearances. I did my best to attempt coordinating the logistics. We coordinated the eventual computer operation out of First Security's offices, using such advance technology as phone modems connecting us to the mainframe at the Harvard Business School, where Rodney ran the data we transmitted to him from the floppy disks couriered from the finish line. Don Facey supplied the race numbers. Bill Squires even pitched in as an impromptu course marshal when the police protection failed to materialize at a key intersection near the North End."

Also in 1977, GBTC won the NU Invitational, the National AAU 20K and the NEAAU Cross-Country. Its two-mile relay was second at the National AAU indoors, and GBTC was third at the National AAU 10,000. At the U.S. Coast Guard Relays, Doyle set a two-mile record of

Tom Grilk. *Photo by Paul C. Clerici.*

8:46.02, and an AR of 10:56 was set in the family relay (Tom Doherty, Pat
Doherty, Mike Doherty and Tim Doherty). Individually, Hodge ran a 4:11
mile at the Dartmouth Relays; Fleming was fifth in the Boston Marathon
(2:18:37); and Rodgers won the Amsterdam Marathon (CR 2:12:47),
Falmouth Road Race (CR 32:23), New York City Marathon (2:11:20,

with Thomas sixth at 2:15:51 in his 26.2-mile debut), Fukuoka Marathon (2:10:55.3), Japan's Kyoto Marathon (2:14:25) and the Waynesboro Marathon (2:25:12). With five wins in six marathons, Rodgers once again was ranked first in the United States and the world by *Track & Field News*. He was joined by Thomas at seventh.

In December, Dillon, a future Big East indoor 3,000-meter champion and All-American harrier, came to GBTC in a similar fashion as most of the members. It was a club for which you fought, struggled and scratched, and that was just the day-to-day off the track. For Dillon, it all started when Thomas and Fleming regaled him with tales of workouts from Rodgers's store on the Boston course in Cleveland Circle. The PC Friar had trained a bit with Thomas, who shared an apartment with Fleming.

"I remember that I spoke with [Squires] for quite a while at the store after a run," Dillon recalls. "I listened while the guys all started asking him what they were going to do the next day. Well, I ended up staying and sleeping on the floor of Randy and Vinnie's apartment for several months." When Dillon later worked for the nearby New Balance factory, "I was actually making shoes for about $3.50 per hour. I could afford one Pino's Pizza a day [and] what I didn't eat at night I had cold for breakfast. I'd give the few cents I had left over to Randy and Vinnie to help for rent. I was usually doing an easy run to work in the morning, sniffing glue fumes all day and a harder run home most afternoons. Other days I'd run to BC's indoor track to meet Coach Bill Squires and the rest of the GBTC guys. Or Randy or Vinnie would pick me up after work, and we'd go to Tufts indoor track."

In just two months, Dillon's presence was felt at the 1978 U.S. Cross-Country Trials. He and Thomas battled to a razor-thin finish, with the former clocked at 35:41.8 (first) and the latter 35:42.1 (second). Rodgers came in seventh (35:45.9) and secured the team title. "Bill Rodgers, Randy and I were leading most of the race, and we were hoping for the three-way tie that morning. Billy had been more focused on just using the race as part of his winter preparation for the BAA [Boston] Marathon," said Dillon. "With a little over a mile to go, we noticed a few non-GBTC guys gaining on us, so Randy and I had to leave Billy, who ended up still nailing down one of the other spots on the team. That was the day I began to think of myself as a 'worthy.' Although I'd already run well enough to make NCAA All-American for Providence, my confidence at high-level competition was still a little shaky sometimes."

Dillon's grassroots approach fit right in. Because whether it was running to and from work, picking up toll-booth loose change en route to away meets, pitching in a few extra dollars to whomever was driving to cover wear and tear, stuffing ten to a hotel room or driving hundreds of miles or several hours to make the weekly workouts, that was what was done at GBTC.

"It was just fun," recalled Meyer of the overall club atmosphere. "I remember when Randy Thomas was in the passenger seat, [at tollbooths] he would want to hook-shot the coins over [the car] to land in the basket, and they'd be clunking all over the place. And at a race in Miami, I had to room with Squires. We walk in, and there's this one big bed with a mirror up on the ceiling above it. I said, 'Baloney! I'm on the floor. Give me a blanket,'" he laughed. Added Pfrangle, "Of course, everyone talks about Coach's wackiness: his predictability—losing track of the time on the stopwatch, getting lost driving to races, looking for change on the streets on runs—and his unpredictability—running a sub-sixty-second 440 in street shoes, an overcoat and a pipe in his mouth. We would all agree, though, that his passion, his commitment, his selflessness for the club was extraordinary. And it was always done with a funny comment, a Squireism of some kind, that always left you scratching your head and thinking, 'What did he say?'"

Thom Gilligan, who became a GBTC president, officer and coach, also noted: "You pursued your passion first and somehow made a living to support your addiction. I lived with Mike Roche, Dave McGillivray, Bob Barnaby and Sharon O'Hagan in a large house at the Boston fifteen-mile mark in Wellesley. There were a few other houses with GBTCers in Newton and Wellesley. We all wanted to train on the famous Boston hills. Most of us knew that we were never going to run 2:10, so we pursued our day jobs with the same passion as we ran the Newton hills during the week and raced the New England road-running circuit on the weekends. You could look at the front three rows and see twenty-five GBTC teammates. You knew with whom you would battle that day. It was about time and place. No one cared about a finisher's medal. If you got some water at the five-mile mark of a ten-miler on a hot summer day, that was more than you expected."

Although during this time, some prizes were worth it. Rodgers won everything from dinners and overnight hotel stays to a watch and a sewing machine. Mark Duggan noted, "A Gardner race was sponsored by a furniture company, and I still have a rocking chair that I won." Doyle recalled a Lowell race in which he came in sixth and won a Sears gift certificate: "It was $200. That was 1975! That was a lot of money. I also won a microwave, the first one we ever had. But New England took a lot of its structure from England, because in England that's what they did—merchandise prizes."

At the 1978 IAAF World Cross-Country 12K Championships in Scotland—won by Ireland's John Treacy, a PC teammate of Dillon's—the United States was second with Meyer third (twentieth overall in 40:31), Rodgers fifth (forty-fourth in 41:20), Thomas ninth (ninety-ninth in 42:54). "I came down with mono on just about the same day my passport arrived in the mail and never made the trip," said Dillon. "I was heartbroken, both not to have been there with Randy and Billy and also not to be able to see the look on John's face after winning the race we all believed to be the hardest one in the world to win."

Meyer, who moved to Boston in 1978 and worked at Rodgers's store, relished training with such a stellar cast. "I focused on the roads, anything from 5K, five miles, up through 25K. And Billy would throw my name to the race directors if he couldn't go to a race. I got all his crumbs! I was a happy guy! Billy knew what my abilities were, but I hadn't created a name yet. My first year I hit the roads, I raced twenty-two weekends in a row trying to make a little money and create a name for myself," said Meyer, who for early recognition points to his ARs at the Fifth Third River Bank 25K in Michigan and the Diet Pepsi 10K in Boston, when he edged his friend. "Beating Bill over Heartbreak Hill [in the 10K] was fun. But it was fine. Billy fully expected me to try to beat him, and he always tried to beat me. Bill and I were lucky with that. We complemented each other pretty well. He was the distance guy and he would join me in the track work. It helped us both."

GBTC won the 1978 National AAU 20K (Thomas first, Mark Duggan fourth, Graham seventh, George Reed tenth and Gary Wallace eleventh), National AAU 20K and the NEAAU Cross-Country (Meyer first, Hodge second, Bob Hensley third, Graham fourth and Paul Oparowski sixth) and was the Gold Medal Team in the National AAU One-Hour Run, which Rodgers won with an AR of 12 miles and 1,350 yards that was second-best in the world. GBTC also came in second at the NEAAU outdoors (with wins by George Reed in the 3-mile, Rocco Petitto in the javelin and Doyle's third-place 4:12.6 mile that was the fastest GBTC mile of the year), tied for second at the NEAAU indoors (led by wins from Doyle in the mile and Bob McCallum in the triple jump) and was third in the National AAU 10,000 (Meyer first and Dillon eleventh), and the two-mile relay team won the National AAU championships in its fifth attempt.

Rodgers—who was pictured solo on the covers of the February 1978 issue of *Track & Field News* as "King of the Road" and the October 30, 1978 *Sports Illustrated*—was once again by *Track & Field News* ranked number one in the United States (Thomas was third) and second in the world as he continued his onslaught with 1978 wins at the Falmouth Road Race (CR

Greg Meyer setting the 5,000-meter indoor American record at Harvard in 1979. *Kerry Loughman photo, courtesy Bob Sevene.*

32:21), New York City Marathon (2:12:12) and Boston Marathon (2:10:13), where Squires at the age of forty-five ran a 2:48:29 (for the BAA). GBTC also captured team titles at Boston (Rodgers in first, Jack Fultz in fourth, Thomas in fifth) and New York (Rodgers in first, George Reed in twenty-ninth, Oparowski in thirty-fourth).

"I trained with Rodgers and all the Greater Boston guys, and I'd do all the track workouts; and we'd end up over at the Eliot. For some reason, I don't remember ever donning a singlet to represent the club in a major competition. I may have in some of the local and regional races, but I'm very much a spiritual part of the team," recalled Fultz, who prior to GBTC won the 1976 Boston Marathon clad in a Georgetown University singlet. One of the few GBTCers who met a U.S president (when he was inducted into his university Hall of Fame in 1996 and enjoyed an event-related run with President Bill Clinton), he also recalled club workouts at the old BC track: "Oh, yeah, the unofficial-sized track that was only about 420 yards long, and it went behind the stands and had some

Bill Rodgers at the 1977 Litchfield Hills Road Race. *Photo by Leo Kulinski Jr.*

frost heaves in it. Should have been condemned, but it was good enough for us. We'd warm up around the reservoir on Tuesday nights, banging out a whole series of 800 meters with a group of us, and by the last couple, Rodgers and I were duking it out; well, just short of a race because we kind of knew better. But still, competitive juices were flowing. But I would use those as markers for where I was."

The summer of 1978 featured an amazing feat of endurance and benevolence by McGillivray. Covering over 40 miles a day for eighty straight days, he ran from Oregon to Massachusetts in Run Across America, in which he raised money for the Jimmy Fund and the Dana-Farber Cancer Institute in Boston. He covered 3,452 miles from Medford to Medford and finished inside Fenway Park in front of 32,000 Red Sox fans before the game on Jimmy Fund Night. McGillivray soon joined GBTC. "Happened right after I ran across the country in 1978," he recalled. "As Coach says, after running 3,452 miles in eighty days, I certainly had my

Dave McGillivray. *Courtesy Dave McGillivray.*

base (mileage) down! For me, it was 100 percent the speedwork on the track at BC. I could always run forever, but I lacked 'speed.' Coach really helped me be able to run close to 5:00-minute pace for anything under 10 miles and 5:30 pace for everything over 10 miles."

In 1979, GBTC won the New England indoors and outdoors, National AAU 20K Cross-Country, NEAAU Cross-Country (Meyer 1st, Dillon 2nd and Hodge 3rd), Canadian 12K Cross-Country Championship and the U.S. Cross-Country Trials (Dillon 5th and Thomas 7th, with Bill Gillin, Hodge, Tim Donovan and Doyle also competing). At the IAAF World Cross-Country 12K Championships in Ireland, Dillon was 44th (38:59), Meyer 90th (39:48) and Thomas 137th (40:45). Recalled Dillon of the IAAF: "The feeling of disappointment [from 1978] left me even more determined to make the team again the next year. [The 1979 race] was one of the most amazing athletic competitions I have ever witnessed. John Treacy successfully defended his title in an amazingly muddy race. He had to be rescued from the hoards of fans filled with national pride who rushed out of the stands and onto the course to try to congratulate him. The officials had a difficult time keeping the fans from ruining the rest of the race for the other runners who had yet to finish."

GBTC's crown jewel came in Raleigh, North Carolina, when it finally won the 1979 National AAU Senior Men's Cross-Country 10,000-Meter Championship. After finishing seventh (1975), ninth (1976) and third (1977–78), Squires realized this was perhaps one of the last chances to win with so much talent onboard before his top guys started taking shoe company contracts. Squires commented: "Yeah, there was talk that [members] were going to be pros. And to be truthful, I kind of think they knew it was going to be the end. I kept saying this team championship [achievement] is all over with. They'll all be individuals with agents and being sent all over the place. I said, 'Guys, this is the biggest thing! I want you to win this freakin' thing!' They were going to work together in groups. I'm going to have Al [Salazar] as the leader—he was used to running on grass. It was almost all grass. And we were going to work three groups. We were in the mecca of distance running in America. We were the unknown of that group. These were all stars and it had taken me almost four years, picking up one or two kids per year. This was it!"

It was total dominance as GBTC took first, third, fourth, fifth and twelfth to win with a meet record (MR) of 26 points (second place scored 179). "You had to declare your first team beforehand, and you could throw it away. But I knew our second group would have won the nationals! Our second team!" exclaimed Squires.

Leaving no doubt, Salazar won in 30:27.8. "It was exciting to win a team championship with all my old friends from Boston," he noted. "I'd won a team championship at Oregon, but Boston was where I'd started, so it was great to win individually but even more fun to be able to celebrate a team championship with my close Boston friends. The 1979 championship was a highlight."

Hodge was third (30:52.6), Dillon fourth (30:56.6), Meyer fifth (31:01.9) and Thomas twelfth (31:23.9). Meyer said about the race: "To me, in terms of a show of force, at a period of time when the club systems across the country were strong—Atlanta, Club Northwest, Colorado Track Club—and you get these guys together and you score twenty-six points? We kicked their asses! There was not a big strategy. It was a strategy that Colorado Track Club was…"talking." There were bets flying back and forth because that was the Shorter group (CTC) and the Bill Rodgers group (GBTC). It was all about beating them. We were lucky that that year Salazar came and ran for our club. I was the national champ the year before, and I was the fourth man on the team and fifth place in the race! I thought I had a bad race, and I got fifth! I wanted to win! You go into the race, you think you're winning! It doesn't always work that way, but when you're running for a team, you don't shut down. I was kicking down against Steve Scott, who got seventh. When you're running for the team, it means something different. Randy Thomas was our fifth man in twelfth, and we gave him grief that he couldn't break the top ten! We were laughing. And Danny? He busted his ass to beat you. He was tough! And Hodgie! They were just hard racers. They knew how to race."

Mark Duggan added, "That's where Squires was really good. Going to a race with a strategy, either to win because the race was important for one reason or another—it was a New England championship, it was points for a team—you had a strategy, for the most part, going in. Even if you didn't think you could win, if there were points involved, what would your best place be? That was a strategy. And he would also have races where you could run for time. Having a strategy was really helpful."

So deep with talent was GBTC at the nationals that future U.S. Olympians Pete Pfitzinger and Bruce Bickford were out of the scoring. "[This] was a highlight for the team, and at the time, for me," noted Pfitzinger of the national title. "I was twenty-fifth and happy to have made the top [six for GBTC]. I was technically on the 'B' team." Fortuitously, when Pfitzinger moved from New York to Boston and joined GBTC in the summer of 1979, he experienced great success almost immediately. "GBTC was the best club in the country. I lived over the Bill Rodgers Running Center in Cleveland Circle with Dave Ezersky. I wanted to learn all I could and was delighted to be able to do some training with GBTC guys, including Bob Hodge, Vin Fleming, Dick Mahoney and Tom Derderian. And occasionally with Bill

Mark Duggan winning the Fort Lauderdale Road Race, despite the Perrier banner stating it's Falmouth. *Courtesy Mark Duggan.*

himself or Greg Meyer. And to join in some of Coach Squires's group track sessions at BC. Everyone was very welcoming of a kid from upstate New York. I learned heaps, and made great friends."

The national title was on the heels of another dominant performance when in April an astonishing four GBTC members finished in the top ten of the 1979 Boston Marathon with Rodgers first (CR 2:09:27), Hodge third (2:12:30), Thomas eighth (2:14:12) and Dick Mahoney tenth (2:14:36). "Compared to all those other guys, I was not nearly as fast or as talented as them. But we got stronger with the workouts we did. We built up," said Dick Mahoney, who also added an approximate 5 miles a day at his day job as a mailman. "But I had trained unbelievably hard that year for Boston. I used to do huge mileage—in excess of 150 miles a week!" Not surprisingly, GBTC won its second straight team title. And the finish-line announcer was Grilk, who has continued that duty ever since, even in his capacity as BAA executive director. Another first was a GBTC member in a tuxedo, which

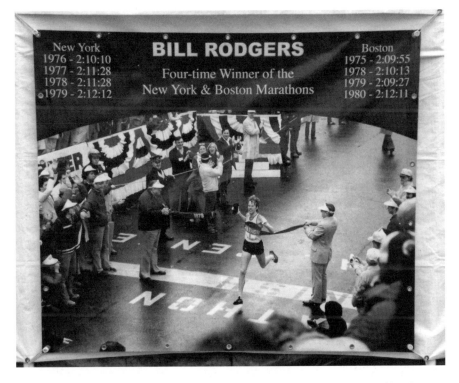

Attached to the side of a merchandise tent during the Boston Marathon weekend can often be seen this large poster of Bill Rodgers winning the 1979 Boston Marathon. *Photo by Paul C. Clerici.*

was something of note in and of itself, having dinner with President Jimmy Carter. After the Boston win, both winners—Rodgers and non-GBTCer Joan Benoit Samuelson—were invited to the White House to attend a state dinner (sixteen years later, Rodgers and Samuelson also shared a run with President Clinton in D.C.).

For Hodge, this was also a highlight year for him as both an individual and a teammate. "The national cross-country in 1979 where we won the team title because we had been trying for it since 1974. It was a great group," he said. And "the turning point for me was the 1979 Boston Marathon where I finished third in 2:12:30, improving on my previous best [of] a forty-sixth place in 1977 Boston in 2:28:45."

One of the crucial elements of GBTC's success were the groups incorporated by Squires, who had dug into his past and created three based on talent level: Group 1 (elites), Group 2 (point-getters who could win and move up) and Group 3 (everyone else). While each group received the same training, it would be tailored in accordance to ability. "The club had a huge number of talented runners with great high school and collegiate careers," said Thom Gilligan. "Bill had won Boston, and everyone with some balls

In the 1979 Boston Marathon, GBTC runners Dick Mahoney (48), Randy Thomas (behind Mahoney) and Bob Hodge (1066), with Garry Bjorklund (15) and Herman Atkins (21). *Courtesy Dick Mahoney.*

wanted to train with him. Thus, the bar was raised very high. You simply thought, 'A 2:09:55 is a very good time for a marathon. I wonder how close I can come to that.' I was on the 'D Team,' in my opinion, with a 2:31 PR. I figured the following: A Team, 2:09–2:18; B Team, 2:19–2:24; C Team, 2:25–2:30; and D Team, 2:30–2:40. We had seventy-two guys at one time who could break 2:40. You would show up at BC on a Sunday morning or at Bill's shop on a summer evening and go for a run...starting at 7:00 pace and ending at race pace [of] 5:00–5:30. You might get dropped off the back of the pack, but you kept fighting to improve."

Don Ricciato (3011) and Jack McDonald (2716) in the 1977 Boston Marathon. *Courtesy Jack McDonald.*

Added Rodgers, "Beyond Coach, the key to our success was our team focus, and that kept getting stronger with new racers like [when] Greg Meyer joined the team, as well as Mike Roche—1976 Olympian in the steeple—and other leaders like Thom Gilligan and Dave McGillivray and Tom Grilk [who] became some of the club's strongest supporters and hardest workers as well as visionaries who worked together creating the Freedom Trail Road Race."

With the groups came the sharks and the guppies, the hunters and the prey, the smart ones and the, well, gullible. The longer an athlete stayed at GBTC, the more Squires's appellations could be heard, such as his ranking of "wacks, sturdleys, goobers, nerdlings, seedlings." And if ever in doubt, do not ask Coach to define, for obvious reasons. Meyer describes an occasion when Roche "was talking with my former wife, Paula, and they used to laugh because most people couldn't understand Squires. And she'd say to Mike, 'I'm starting to worry about Greg because he actually understands him.' And I could!" he said with a laugh and added on a serious note, "I knew what

Tom Grilk in his capacity as Boston Athletic Association executive director. *Photo by Paul C. Clerici.*

he was trying to communicate. I knew what he was trying to accomplish with the training. As goofy as he was at times—I mean, he'd be sitting there reading the paper, thinking he's reading intervals off, and we're just laughing because he's nowhere close—it didn't matter because it's about the work. It wasn't about the time, it was about the work. And he knew."

The small club was beginning to expand, whether it wanted to or not. No longer was GBTC strictly for track and field. Along with the national running boom—primarily ignited by Shorter's 1972 Olympic Marathon gold and Rodgers's 1975 Boston Marathon win—runners of all kinds began to take notice and join clubs to compete at all levels. "It was an evolving thing," recalled Jack McDonald. "When I left (in 1977–78), I was sort of the centerpiece for that track-and-field kind of thing. And then the explosion of Rodgers, Salazar, Hodge, Thomas, Dick Mahoney [all in the marathon], and they required a lot of attention by Coach, by the media. But every Tuesday night, we all trained together." Sevene added, "The club changed to more of a distance racing club, but with the guidance of Bill Squires and the success of Greg Meyer, Dan Dillon, Randy Thomas, Bob Hodge, Dick Mahoney and Vinnie Fleming in both cross-country and the marathon, the GBTC became well-known nationally."

With a growing cross-section of athletes, who ran everything from the 100 to the marathon, Squires employed great creativity to his training sessions, some of which he learned as a runner himself. One road workout had his athletes alternate stride length while running from utility pole to utility pole and increasing the distance from every other pole to every two poles, then three

At the 1979 Litchfield Hills Road Race. *From left*: Amby Burfoot (7) and GBTC runners Bob Hodge (1066), Walter Murphy (637), Dave McGillivray (9) and Tom Grilk (5). *Photo by Leo Kulinski Jr.*

and so on. Another workout would find Squires in his parked car ahead of the pack, and as they reached him, he'd yell out the change of pace and then drive ahead to a distance unknown to the runners, who would continue that pace until they saw him again for the next command. He surmised the changing distances and speeds replicated race experience.

"I liked doing longer runs that had some intensity to them and change of pace," said Meyer. "The things that gained the confidence for me were those hard fartlek twenty-milers that we did [on the Boston Marathon course]," he said in reference to the Swedish word for varying speeds during a workout. "We'd start in Wellesley on the track with a two-mile at about 5:00 race pace. Then you were out on the course, running down towards Cleveland Circle: 2:00 hard, 2:00 easy, 3:00 hard, easy—all the way up with a 10:00 surge in the middle, and then you'd work your way back up. That was all scripted—you knew when you were going again. But we were averaging 5:10, 5:15 a mile, but your fast part much faster and your slow was 5:30, but there were bits in there that you were just crunching it. And you went back up the hills to Wellesley and then finished on the track with a mile or two. Brutal. That busted my ass."

Women began to make a name for themselves toward the end of the 1970s. When some of his female students at Boston State College began to inquire about running, Squires invited them—and others—to run with the club. The workouts began to yield good results and places in various races, including for Sue Lupica, who in 1978 came in fifty-seventh (40:30) out of five thousand runners in the New York Women's Mini-Marathon 10K and fourteenth (39:18) in the Beverly 10,000-Meter Run for Women and ran a 3:23 marathon debut at the Lowell Classic. At the 1979 NEAAU 15K Women's Road Racing Championship, GBTC was led by Linda Lecoq in tenth (1:01:57), with Mary Ann Bray, Margaret Champion, Pam Duckworth, Frannie (Fisher) Hodge, Lori Sparks, Norma Ligor, Diana Dickinson and Sandy Miller also in the race. Women were also beginning to run in more races, including the Bonne Bell Mini Marathon in Boston, which was, at the time, reportedly one of a dozen women-only races in the United States. The Bonne Bell, which would become known as the Tufts Health Plan 10K for Women, started in 1977.

Said Duckworth of the NEAAU, "I ran the 1979 15K in 1:04:57 and placed 23rd out of 114, but I noted [in my log] that I was disappointed with my performance. The weather was perfect, and I was psyched; but I didn't perform up to my expectations. The GBTC women's team was third, only twenty-seven seconds behind second-place CSU." At another NEAAU 15K a few years later, Duckworth does recall an instance that involved teammate Sharon (O'Hagan) Gilligan and a certain professional Boston sports hero. "After the race, I did the cool-down with a few teammates [for] maybe 2 or 2.5 miles, and then we went back to the finish area to relax. Sharon must have been training for a marathon because she wanted to do more miles after the race than the rest of us, so she continued running by herself. Finally, the effects of the race caught up with her, and she felt exhausted and unable to run anymore; but she was alone in a residential area where she knew no one. There were no cell phones in those days." (O'Hagan) Gilligan continued, "It was a bad idea. I suddenly became very dizzy, weak, and felt like I was going to pass out. I laid down on this guy's lawn for a while and then went to the backdoor for help." It was the home of future NBA Hall of Fame Boston Celtic Dave Cowens, who along with his wife came to her aid. "Dave Cowens was so nice. They gave me water and then, when I was a little better, gave me a ride back [to the race site]."

The 1970s closed out with a few changes for GBTC—Larry Newman as managing director, Grilk as vice-president, Facey as treasurer and

Wendy Cully and Lupica as secretary and women's events; several committees were formed for track and field, road racing, men's masters, special events, social and newsletter; and the coaching staff added Sevene (track and field advisor/coach).

The headquarters/offices would depend on whose residence it would be housed in. Meetings were also held at headquarters and on occasion the Exchange Restaurant, with various holiday parties at BC's Philomatheia Club or the Eliot Lounge. "The Eliot was probably as close to a clubhouse as we had at the time, which made Tommy Leonard de facto a huge part of the club," said McGrath of the pub that also housed Squires, who'd calculate workouts and deliver his soliloquies. "We established Coach's Corner at the end of the bar," said Leonard. "When all the visiting runners came in, he would hold court. You never knew when the sentences were going to end or where he's coming from. But he just held the crowd." Noted Mark Duggan, who won Nantucket's inaugural 1976 Columbus Day 10-Mile Road Race (the weekend of which included travel to the race via a boat, plane and police escort and featured high winds and rain and a post-race dinner next to Senator Edward Kennedy, due to Leonard), "Having the epicenter be the Eliot, everybody wanted

Larry Newman. *Photo by Paul C. Clerici.*

In Canada for its marathon and track events. *Standing, from left*: Kevin Crowley, Scott Graham, Pat Doherty, Mark Duggan and Glen Charbonneau; *sitting, from left*: Ken Graham and Mike Doherty. *Courtesy Fred Doyle.*

to have the high-profile guys at their races, and Tommy would always be the one [asked] at the bar. Every now and then, he'd get Rodgers to come, but then if he couldn't, and you were there, Tommy would get us in." Adds Doyle, "He was incredibly nice to us. He got us in more races, fixed us up with places to say, always talked about us, so all these people would open up their homes to us."

The nascent club began to struggle to stay ahead of its own popularity and growth.

Chapter Two

1980–1989

H eading into the 1980s with such a great track (and cross-country and road-race) record, it was naturally expected that GBTC would only get better and tougher. And it did.

The 1979–80 indoor season closed out with a cache of greatness. In January alone, GBTC shined throughout the Dartmouth Relays and won the NEAAU with a thirty-seven-point cushion, where one of the Men's Outstanding Performance trophy honors went to Meyer, whose 13:45.58 win in the 5,000 was the second fastest in the United States. At the Brooks Indoor Track Invitational inside the Houston Astrodome, New England records fell in the 5,000 (13:44.19 by Bickford) and the two-mile relay (7:26.79 by Rich Nichols, John Demers, Keith Francis and Rich Puckerin). GBTC also won the New England indoors for its fourth title in seven years; Dillon was second at the U.S. Cross-Country Trials; and Thomas won Japan's prestigious Ohme-Hochi 30K.

"A truly great experience, as the Japanese hosts have always been extremely gracious," Thomas noted of the 30K, which he ran with Hodge. After the race, the teammates relaxed in an old hotel at the foot of the Hakone Mountains. "Looking out large glass windows, at water level, and at the base of Mount Fuji, I turned to Hodgie and said, 'Hodgie, this is something we will remember for the rest of our lives.'"

Just five months after his 3,452-mile run, McGillivray at the 1980 Hawaii Ironman Triathlon finished in fourteenth (11:33:28). In the ensuing few years, he would add to his massive mileage and fundraising with unique

Dan Dillon (76) and Randy Thomas (37) at Harvard in 1980. *Kerry Loughman photo, courtesy Bob Sevene.*

events in 1980, including the East Coast Run (1,520 miles with Bob Hall) and Wrentham State School 24-Hour Run (120 miles); 1981, the New England Run (1,522 combined run/bike/swim miles); and 1983, the Jimmy Fund 24-Hour Swim (26.2 miles in 1,884 laps). His highlight? "For me, it was traveling out to Oregon with the team [for the] Nike-OTC Marathon with the hope of qualifying for the Trials. I, of course, failed at that, but it was a highlight of my running career to be on the same track at the same time with all the studs," said McGillivray, who became the second GBTC athlete in as many years to meet the president, when, during the East Coast Run, he was greeted by President Carter at the White House (twenty-three years later, he would also meet President Barack Obama during a post–Boston Marathon visit).

Dave McGillivray finishing the 1979 Boston Marathon. *Courtesy Dave McGillivray.*

As an Olympic year, all eyes were on the 1980 outdoor season and the Trials in preparation for the XXII Olympiad in Moscow. Squires was named U.S. Olympic 10K/marathon coach, and every workout, competition and goal was in place to peak for the Trials and Games. However, Squires grew concerned about news of a foreign invasion of military forces in Afghanistan by the Soviet Union. As a coach, he received updates of the December 1979 events, which quickly mushroomed into an international political situation where a boycott was being discussed as a possibility. While Squires maintained his coaching schedule, it became a *fait accompli* when the Soviet Union refused to withdraw its troops by a U.S.-set deadline. As a result, it was announced on March 21 that the United States would boycott the Moscow Summer Games (the boycott eventually included sixty-five countries). As the timing of the boycott came before the Trials were run, athletes pondered whether or not to compete since there would be no advancement to the Games.

Rodgers, who spoke publicly about his displeasure of the boycott, won the 1980 Boston Marathon (2:12:11) with a death threat aimed at him that said he'd be targeted by mile twenty-four (in a show of both defiance

Bill Squires runs alongside Bill Rodgers during the 1980 Boston Marathon. *Jeff Johnson photo, courtesy Bill Squires.*

and support, Squires ran alongside Rodgers on a portion of the course, dispensing water and encouragement). Rodgers also chose not to run in the U.S. Olympic Trials Marathon. And he was not alone. Of the 225 qualifiers, 33 (by choice, injury, etc.) did not toe the line. GBTC had 7 qualifiers in Doyle (DNF), Hodge, Dick Mahoney, Oparowski (2:20:28.3), Rodgers, Thomas (seventh at 2:13:39.6) and Wallace (2:24:43.4). "Of course I was bitterly disappointed, as you never want to see politics interfere with the holy grail of athletics," remarked Thomas. "But I made a decision to move forward with my training as planned. Competing in an Olympic Team Trial, despite the watered-down entry list, was a remarkable experience."

As a result of the boycott, Squires was informed that, as a concession, he could travel to any race he wanted to for free. Thomas, who'd been invited to run the 1981 Tokyo Marathon, thought that decision an easy one. "Before we left the States, I reminded him to bring some gifts for our hosts, as they are traditionally so generous," recalled Thomas, who added that Squires, as was his wont, forgot. "On the way to the airport, he ducked into a pharmacy, went to the back shelves and bought a package of 8 x 10 cardboard squares—paid $1.80—with some crazy Chinese proverbs printed on each, such as 'He who spits in wind spits in own face.' Upon his arrival in Tokyo, he was showered with gifts, ranging from a beautiful watch to a great sound system. And, of course, he reciprocated by handing out his Chinese proverbs." After Thomas came in third (2:12:31), they had dinner thirty-five stories above Tokyo, surrounded by all glass that offered priceless vistas of the capital city. "During our meal, and, of course, starting immediately following the finish of the race, Coach was talking in his normal animated fashion, about only god knows what. Finally, I looked at him and said, 'Wack, stop talking and look around you. We are looking over one of the greatest cities in the world, eating an excellent meal. We have life by the balls. Try to take it all in.'"

For the track and field qualifying heats and Trials, GBTC fielded Tom Mahan (110-meter hurdles), Meyer and Roche (3,000-meter steeplechase), Dillon and Salazar (5,000 and 10,000). In the heats, Mahan (fifth at 14:24 in the third quarterfinal) missed advancing by just 0:31. Roche (fourth at 8:31.50 in the first) and Meyer (second at 8:28.34 in the second) both advanced. Dillon (fourth at 13:53.45 in the 5,000 second) advanced, but Salazar (seventh at 13:46.51 in the 5,000 first) did not. In the Trials, Roche was seventh (8:32.34), Meyer ninth (8:40.7), Dillon sixth in the 5,000 (13:41.58), Salazar third in the 10,000 (28:10.42) and Dillon fifteenth in the 10,000 (28:57.5).

Of his Trials, Dillon noted, "[In the 10K] I dropped well back—probably even got lapped—by the end, and a tactical dual developed between Herb Lindsay and Craig Virgin. Alberto hung in there for most of it. The next day I was a little tired, but since I'd also qualified for the 5K, I ran the semifinals and somehow made it through. I felt much better two days later in the 5K finals. I think nerves got the better of me in the 10K, and by the end of the 5K rounds, I wasn't afraid anymore."

On the track, in field events and on the roads, GBTC continued to make waves. "We trained at all levels," stated Rodgers. "We were a track team as well as a road team, and we had fun going to races and celebrating them as well."

At the 1980 National Masters and Sub-Masters indoors, Rip Dyer achieved national champion status in the long jump. At the National AAU outdoors, Doyle ran a 4:09 mile and Bickford set a three-mile AR. At the National TAC (The Athletics Congress) outdoors, All-American honors went to Meyer and Pfitzinger. At the NEAAU 10K, Hodge won (29:42).

GBTC athletes. *Sitting, from left*: Bob Hodge, Tom Doherty, Chuck Riley, Vinnie Fleming and Mike Doherty; *second row*: Todd Miller, Fred Doyle and Pat Doherty; *back row*: Chuck Flanagan, Scott Graham, John Theriault (leaning forward), Mark Duggan and Walter Murphy (kneeling). *Courtesy Fred Doyle.*

GBTC won the New England outdoors, and in August at the NTAC 20K Championships (formerly the NAAU 20K in March), Hodge won (1:02:35) and Wallace came in fifth.

Even with regional and national wins, workouts were still held in high regard and not taken lightly, even if not always favorably. Recalled Pfitzinger: "The most difficult workouts did not actually help me. They were an 800-meter

Pete Pfitzinger leading the 1984 U.S. Olympic Marathon Trials. *Photo by Leo Kulinski Jr.*

workout I did with [Rodgers] and a couple of other guys in which I blew up and learned those guys were still a level better than me. And also a workout of 300s with Greg Meyer that took me a week to recover from, as evidenced by a terrible 10,000-meter race about five days later. The most beneficial workouts were the many hour-and-a-half runs up Commonwealth Avenue, learning the craft and mile reps with Dick Mahoney and others. Plus, 'trash hill' with Derderian."

With a chuckle, Derderian explained: "There was a landfill close to my house and a very steep hill of trash with grass growing on it, and we'd do our hill sprints up this hill of trash. And we'd make all kinds of jokes about running on trash, being trashed, trashing ourselves—I mean, you've got to do something while you're running. It was literally a trash hill."

The women also continued to excel. The Women's NEAAU 10K Championships, which also held a 5K beforehand, featured thirteen GBTCers in the 10K, led by Paula Lettis in thirteenth (35:21 PR), and four in the 5K, led by Duckworth (who won her division), Elydia Siegel-Davis and Sandy Macri, all of whom also ran the 10K. At the New England Athletics Congress (NEAC) 15K, Monica Reed led GBTC in twenty-second (1:04:32); and at the first annual Etonic/NEAC Women's 25K Road Racing Championship in 1980, nicknamed the "Wonder Woman 25K," GBTC A (Bray, Cynthia Hastings and Francine DeGrande) was third and GBTC B (Bridgette Huber, Duckworth and [Fisher] Hodge) fifth.

"The club saw a need for such a race for women only and filled the need," said Hastings of the 25K, which saw two ARs. Added Duckworth, "It was hot and humid—my least favorite conditions—and I had a terrible race; 'one of my worst races ever,' according to my log. What I vaguely remember about that race was that there had not been a U.S. championship race at 25K for several years, so the club was very excited to have the opportunity to host the race. My prerace job was to solicit prizes from local merchants so that there would be good prizes for the winners. And I recall that the merchants were quite generous."

In July, GBTC fielded a group in its first major-level track event at the 1980 Kendall Women's Classic, where they recorded PRs in the submasters mile (6:10 by Duckworth) and 18-and-over mile (5:46 by Bray, 5:49 by Robin Clayton, 6:02 by Dickinson, 6:06 by Hastings and 6:06.5 by DeGrande). Dickinson also ran a 2:56 in the 880 about thirty-five minutes after she ran the mile, and the 1,600-meter relay (Bray, Clayton, Hastings and DeGrande) ran a 5:12.23.

To accommodate the need to handle this influx of interest (and success), GBTC created the Road Racing Committee, which held its first meeting in

Cynthia Hastings. *Courtesy Erin (Cullinane) Kandamar.*

June 1980. Paul Caruccio, Peter Ciraface, Miles Coverdale, Bob Goldszer, Lettis, McGrath, Jan Mitchell and Thomas were responsible for everything from administration and volunteers to travel, prizes and results. Outside the club, members were also in demand. Bill Clark was named an NEAC vice-president. Thomas served on the summer staff of the New England Track and Field Camp. And books from members included an updated version of Squires's 1979 *Improving Your Running* (by Squires and Raymond Krise) in 1981, the detailed *Fast Tracks: The History of Distance Running Since 884 B.C.* by Krise and Squires in 1982 and *Improving Women's Running* also by Squires and Krise in 1983. And to increase its visibility, the club in 1980 began to sell GBTC bumper stickers as well as the usual assortment of singlets, shirts, shorts, warm-up suits, rain suits and running caps, some of which were produced by the Bill Rodgers Running Center's clothing line. In addition, the March 1980 newsletter first called itself the *Wingfoot Express* and featured the ubiquitous winged-foot logo of Hermes, the Greek mythological messenger of the gods.

But the fall of 1980 also held dark days. Within a span of about six months, Bickford, Dillon and Salazar departed for Nike's Athletics West and Tim Donovan, Mark Duggan, Fleming, Graham, Dick Mahoney, Meyer,

Okerman, Andy Palmer, Pfitzinger, Roche and Thomas left for Team New Balance. Rodgers joined the exodus in 1982 for PUMA. "The business of running started to grow," said Mark Duggan. "You'd run and work, but at some point, you had to decide whether you wanted to run at a level nationally or internationally or you're going to work. You couldn't do both because it became a business. Some could make a living running, and then there was the group that could work for a shoe company." Added Doyle, "It became less about the team and the club, and it became more about doing what's best for yourself and your career."

While the reward was a shoe company contract, that achievement wasn't always the point. "At first, that wasn't a goal," recalled Doyle of the early days. "The shoe companies weren't doing that. Nike would sponsor athletes, but you could run for whatever club you wanted to and wear the club jersey and [the shoe company's] warm-ups. And New Balance started giving more to the club. Then all of a sudden, they decided—coming up to 1980—they wanted to start their own clubs. That's when the clubs started to break up."

For Pfitzinger, he points to his years at GBTC as one of the means to his successes. "The turning point was learning from the masters. My apprenticeship the summer of 1979 was invaluable. I learned how to train and the right attitude to succeed. It was that no one workout is important but, rather, success comes from the day-after-day, week-after-week, month-after-month accumulation of adaptations."

On the heels of these losses, and the prospect of advising and honing athletes at New Balance, Squires decided to resign. In an open letter in the October 1980 newsletter, he expressed his appreciation, gratitude, pride and GBTC accomplishments, which included numerous major-city marathon wins, seventeen national titles, six national champions and seven national record-holders, track records, PRs and CRs. He also offered his continued services, albeit not on a daily basis in the capacity as head coach. And he stayed true to his word. To replace him, Squires thought of Dick Mahoney or Sevene, both of whom he believed understood the overall vision of a coach. GBTC went with a coaching staff of Thom Gilligan (Track and Field chairperson), Jim O'Brien (Men's Road Running chairperson) and Lane (Tuesday workouts). They joined Dotty Fine (Women's Road Running chairperson).

"Most guys knew their workouts and ran together once Coach had other obligations," noted Thom Gilligan. "The key was that there was still a large pod of good runners left who trained together. Coach was always around for advice. Everyone knew that they had to form a good distance base of miles and more miles." Added Lane, "Bill Squires had moved on, and I volunteered to push a stopwatch, yell encouragement and be a good listener. I was just an instrument of transition on an interim basis."

Club finances were still a concern. Rodgers—whose stores were in Cleveland Circle, Worcester, Boston—did offer discounts. But as far as fundraising, it still fell on Gurnet and Freedom Trail. The treasury was not prosperous, which was largely due to the fact that Freedom Trail—whose entrance fee increased to five dollars—suffered from inconsistent sponsorship, changing since 1977: Labatt, Hood, OMNI, Saucony and none in 1980. In 1981, when the treasury had dipped severely, the topic of PUMA sponsoring the club was discussed at length. The initial proposal was PUMA clothing and shoes would be provided to self-selected members who would in turn test them and answer questionnaires. Finances most years would dip so low that payment of bills would wait until after Freedom Trail money came in. So severe was the monetary drought in the mid-1980s that, at one time, it was but for only one member's personal loan that kept the club afloat. GBTC was outgrowing itself.

Regarding the club's growing pains, McGrath noted the important issue was "finding funds to support the club and team travel [which] was always one of our biggest challenges. And then maintaining the club after the shoe companies stepped in with clubs of their own, which, of course, lost us some of our best runners—although they always remained GBTCers at heart."

Originally formed for track and field, then infused with great road-racing and long-distance runners, GBTC was at an athletic crossroad. It was changing. For example, members were seen at a dozen marathons in 1980. Marathoners were coming from this *track club*. When Rodgers wrote his 1980 autobiography (with Boston sportswriter Joe Concannon), it was called simply *Marathoning*.

In recognition of what it had in long distance, the club, in 1982, compiled an all-time list of its top one hundred marathon times from those who ran them as a GBTCer. Wheelchair champion Bob Hall led the club with a superb 2:02:21 (1980 Boston). The next nine times were all sub-2:20s, with Rodgers in a CR 2:09:27 (1979 Boston), Salazar in 2:09:41 (1980 New York), Hodge in 2:10:59 (1980 Nike-OTC), Thomas in 2:11:25 (1978 Boston), Rodgers in 2:12:38 (1982 Boston), Dick Mahoney in 2:14:36 (1979 Boston), Tim Donovan in 2:17:49 (1978 Boston), Fleming in 2:18:37 (1977 Boston) and Wallace in 2:18:51 (1979 Nike-OTC).

Women also had a list, with Pat (Meade) Lavelle's 2:57 as GBTC's first female sub-3:00 (1982 Boston) and a 3:01:01 (1981 Boston). "My training prior to the 1982 Boston," noted (Meade) Lavelle, who married Tom "TL" Lavelle in 1984, "consisted of weekly track and hill workouts along with ten-, twelve-, eighteen- or twenty-mile runs on Sunday. My weekly mileage ranged from sixty to seventy-five miles per week." The list continued with Mary Ann Gedritis in 3:04:23 (1981 Cape Cod), Fine in 3:09:35 (1981 Newport), Jean Smith in 3:09:41 (1981 Foxboro), Bray in 3:11:00 (1980 Foxboro), (O'Hagan) Gilligan in 3:11:56 (1981 Newport), Duckworth in 3:13:09 (1981 Foxboro), Mitchell in 3:13:30 (1981 Foxboro), Dianne Schmitt in 3:13:38 (1982 Boston), (Fisher) Hodge in 3:16:40 (1980 Foxboro), Monica Reed in 3:17 (1980 Casco Bay), (O'Hagan) Gilligan in 3:17 (1982 Boston), Schmitt in 3:18:21 (1981 Newport), Champion in 3:27:57 (1978 Newport), Maureen Rasp in 3:28:04 (1978 Skylon), Kathy Vieweg in 3:29:41 (1981 Newport), Fine in 3:29:42 (1982 Boston), Ligor in 3:29:57 (1980 Foxboro) and Hastings in 3:30:00 (1978 Boston).

"My favorite race was always the Boston Marathon," said Duckworth, who joined GBTC in 1979. "I had started running in 1975, when I graduated from law school and needed an efficient way to get a mental and physical break from working. I met a group of women through the club, and having running partners and coaches really helped maximize my running performances and my enjoyment of the sport. Our Sunday long runs were my favorites and were a critical part of marathon training. Each week, we would meet at a different person's home or apartment, run the route the hostess had planned and then regroup for coffee and brunch and socializing. These were great bonding experiences and I always planned my weekend around them."

Fine recalls 1981 as a year in which she recorded some of her best and worst times (races and otherwise). "It turned out to be a strange and wonderful year for me, and the height of my running. Strangely enough, the year started off with some PRs for me (including) a 6:10 mile at the GBTC Invitational. Here, the strange part kicks in—a team member, Sandy Miller, and I got hit by a car while cooling down in Washington Park. Sandy needed major surgery on her leg. My fat, little butt turned purple and hurt; like being whipped if I tried to run. But I was back running soon and doing PRs at many distances." At the Bonne Bell 10K, "I was primed to really cut loose. And what really got my adrenaline going was being knocked down at the start! I was furious and pulled myself up, looking disgustingly at my ripped, brand-new glitter gloves and my scraped palms and knees, and took off and never looked back."

An addendum to that women's list was Jean Smith, who before the end of the year ran GBTC's second sub-3:00 time with a 2:58 at the 1982 Ocean State in Newport, Rhode Island. "I remember Newport as a wonderful run, where I did not realize until the last few miles that I was running first and alternately second! It was a glorious day. I was fairly new to running and had done many months of pretty high mileage, as I recall. The awards ceremony was so very disappointing, with the second- and third-place men getting shoes and clothing and weekend lodging in Newport. I was given a wicker hamper with old tee shirts from the previous several years! Can you imagine?"

GBTC had morphed into a club of over four hundred, thanks, in large part, to the membership form having been—perhaps mistakenly—printed on the back of the Freedom Trail application. "For years, you didn't know how to get in the club. Somebody had to ask you. Then all of a sudden, the doors opened and we'd go to the workouts and wonder who these people were," Doyle recalled with a laugh.

Nearly a quarter of the membership was women, who were able to avail themselves of specific workouts by Newman. He scheduled Heartbreak Hill repeats, BC campus runs, track intervals, recovery and tapering miles and long runs. "The workouts were indeed grueling. And at times I would feel sick to my stomach all day, knowing what was in store for me that night," acknowledged (O'Hagan) Gilligan. "But when I realized the rewards of such hard work, I kept at it. Looking back at my favorite workouts, I have to say doing ladders, time trials and the Developmental Meets we would have at BC every second Wednesday are certainly highlights. Hill workouts were a close second, as they built strength, which helped injury prevention."

Hastings agreed, "The track workouts were very important to me. The workouts were hard, and I was on edge on Mondays and Tuesdays. After the Wednesday workout, I could relax and the rest of the week flew by." Jean Smith also enjoyed the camaraderie and noted, "Having been a pre–Title IX woman, I had not known what it meant to really train, to be coached, to have fierce women competitors as my teammates. I remember my first marathon with the GBTCers—the old Foxboro Marathon—with Pam Duckworth and Frannie (Fisher) Hodge and Dotty Fine. We ran hard and supported one another regardless of the order in which we finished. It was a sweet time." Norma Deprospo recalled of her recruitment, "Back in 1977, when I started running, I met Dotty for the first time. She introduced herself and asked if I would be interested in joining [GBTC]. If it [hadn't been] for Dotty, I would not have met all of [them]. I have many wonderful memories."

Around this time, Mark Reytblat was named GBTC's new track and field coach. A top Ukraine sprinter from the University of Leningrad, he was a BU assistant coach and a licensed massage therapist. The continued growth of the club also required a large Wingfoot Express Newsletter Committee staff, which was soon replaced by the Communications Group that would absorb its duties as well as take charge of any public relations–related responsibilities.

Despite its financial matters and growth spurts, in 1981, GBTC won the NEAC men's indoors for the third consecutive year and fifth time in eight years, the New England men's outdoors for the third straight year and fifth time in eight years and the NEAAU 20K for the ninth consecutive year. In 1982, with meet directors Newman, Jim O'Brien and Okerman, the club held the inaugural New Balance/GBTC Invitational Track and Field Meet. But one of the club's most storied records—nine straight NEAAU/TAC 20K team titles—saw its end in 1983 when GBTC chose not to send a team. The reason(s), as expressed in a detailed open letter delivered to the TAC Convention, was the board's disappointment with the organizer's lack of quality races, professionalism, and respect for the event in recent years.

This was also a time of frustration and uncertainty. With its purpose uncertain (a club for track and field, road races, trail races, marathons, triathlons, ultras); member involvement seemingly stagnant (poor attendance at annual meetings where votes were taken and awards handed out and only six members having completed a recent informational questionnaire); members forgoing weekly workouts and requesting individual ones; club singlets not being worn at races; reportedly unhinged leadership with noted heated and uneasy relations on the board, GBTC lacked organization and a long-term vision. There was also concern voiced in the newsletter—justified or not—regarding lower-echelon members, who with slower times and reportedly less talent were allegedly tainting the club's premium name. If there was any doubt about the sentiment, it was all laid out in the *Wingfoot Express*. At the following annual election, though, the board remained basically unchanged, as did the officers. The separate men's and women's track and field committees, however, were combined into one GBTC Track & Field Committee. And with its famous national streak over, seventeen years until another NEAC indoors title and nineteen years before another New England outdoors, it would also be many years of mediocrity on certain levels.

But while internal rumblings continued, GBTC still held its own in some competitions. The club won the 1982 NTAC 40K Race Walk

As part of the 1982 Scarborough Marathon Festival in England (from left) GBTC runners Thom Gilligan, Fred Doyle, Brad Hurst, Rodney Pearson, Gary Wallace and local British TV reporter Guy Williams ride elephants to promote the race. *Courtesy Fred Doyle.*

Championships with Troy Engle (fifth, 3:39:24), Mark Fenton (sixth, 3:40:43) and Steve Vaitones (fourteenth, 3:54:43). Pearson tore up the roads with wins at the 1982 Mississippi Marathon (2:33:44) and Mardi Gras Marathon (2:23), and Cynthia Dauphin was second at the 1982 New Jersey Marathon (3:16). GBTC also sent Doyle, Thom Gilligan, Brad Hurst, Pearson and Wallace across the pond to the Scarborough Festival Marathon on the east coast of England.

Two days before the Scarborough Marathon, the quintet met with the mayor over early morning brandy and were then escorted to the village beachfront for some publicity photos with a herd of elephants from the Robert Brothers Circus for the Scarborough Carnival. Or so they thought. "We get there and they want us to get on the elephants! That was pretty hairy," recalled Doyle. "It gets down on its knees, you climb on, and when the elephant gets up, it's a little wobbly. You pitch forward when it moves. And you can't hold their ears. You have to squeeze your legs." Turns out it was

A victorious Fred Doyle atop British police constable Richard Raine after winning the 1982 Scarborough Marathon in England. *Courtesy Fred Doyle.*

GBTC's first pachyderm race, which included one elephant initially heading toward the North Sea before resuming the contest. "The scariest part was getting off," Doyle recalls. "Gilligan was on this two-story elephant, and he was next to me. When the elephant got down, his started to roll, and he had to scramble to get off."

On race day, while five of the top six spots saw Doyle first (2:19:34), Wallace second (2:21:42), Pearson third (2:24:38), Thom Gilligan fifth (2:30:45) and Hurst sixth (2:31:00), the dominating performance garnered less media ink than the lone Brit—Mike "the Tyke" O'Connell—who snuck in fourth. "The headline the next day was 'O'Connell chases Yanks home.' Barely a mention of us," the winner said with a laugh. "But it was a lot of fun. The people were great to us and treated us really, really nice."

In 1982, Jim Hebert experienced a fine stretch of races with four top-five showings in a month with a second and three fifth places, including being part of a three-teammate domination at the Brewster Brew Run 5.2-miler with Tim Donovan (first) and Bill Okerman (third). "But that is not the highlight," he stated of Brewster. "I grabbed two beers at the finish and was waiting for my roommate to finish the race and would give him a beer as he crossed the line. Alas, he never got the beer, as I spotted a really cute girl wearing a GBTC singlet cross the line before him, and I gave her the beer," he said of spotting the former Susan Stumpf. "We have been married for twenty-six years now."

The 1983 GBTC Invitational, after some doubt as to its continuance, was held once again at Harvard, where more than four hundred athletes competed (Okerman, a meet director, clocked a 4:03.9 mile). Around this time, Meyer, the president of the ARRA (Association of Road Racing Athletes) runners union that contributed to the eventual right for amateur athletes to earn themselves prize money, had already begun to train for the marathon. As he initially came to Boston to become a better runner—not necessarily a marathoner—Meyer benefited from the tutelage of Squires and Sevene. He won the 1980 Detroit Marathon, 1981 Cascade Run Off 15K and 1982 Chicago Marathon (CR 2:10:59) and was ranked sixth in the nation in the marathon by *Track & Field News* in 1982.

"Well," Meyer began with a smile, "the reason I ran the marathon was after I set the American record for 10K, Tommy Leonard said to me at the Eliot one night that one day I could be as good as Vinnie Fleming because Vinnie had run well in Boston. And I thought, 'Damn, you get no respect here unless you run the damn Marathon.' It really was the competitive thing about they'll only treat you like an athlete here if you run the Marathon. The American records didn't matter," he chuckled. But it was the group training that enabled him to grow into a marathoner. "It was the volume of work that you were able to do without mentally burning yourself out because you had so many people helping you carry the load. It was a talented group of guys and it evolved to where more guys came in. The Greater Boston Track Club for a period of years was as good as any distance track club in the world. We beat most countries! It was a special time to be here."

To fine-tune for the 1983 Boston Marathon, Squires subjected Meyer to a wide variety of race distances leading up to race day. Of the ten he ran, which ranged from the mile to 30K, Meyer won eight and set one AR, one CR and three PRs. "You need to get yourself into race shape. You need a couple of really hard tune-ups to get yourself ready for something that's important," Meyer recognized. "And I think that's where the Greater Boston Track Club excelled."

For the 1983 Boston, "It was all about reacting," said Meyer. "The strategy was twofold: don't attack the hills, run the flats in between them—unless it's about breaking somebody. And then all of those surges that we practiced on those tempo runs was really to keep the pace going fast. What Squires had me do—and I remember doing it twice in the first half of the race—was, if the pace felt like it was starting to settle in [and] because I was the favorite they would respond to me, push it for maybe fifty yards. The whole pack would respond; and it would pick the pace back up, and I could tuck back in for a while. And fake surges."

Unlike when Rodgers ran his first Boston as an unknown, there was some attention in the direction of Meyer, who found himself on the cover of the April 1983 debut issue of *Boston Running News*, the forbearer to *New England*

April 1983 debut issue of *Boston Running News* with Greg Meyer on the cover. *Courtesy Bob Fitzgerald of* New England Runner.

Runner. Clad in his GBTC singlet, the cover proclaimed, "Greg Meyer Goes for It All in Boston."

With a 4:55 pace, the twenty-seven-year-old won in a time of 2:09. "Like all great coaches, Squires was able to convey a sense of confidence in his athletes getting ready for Boston," said Meyer, whose 1983 *Track & Field News* ranking in the United States jumped to number two. He continued: "Obviously, his training works for Boston. Look at his track record—Billy, Salazar, Hodgie, Randy—he knows what he's doing. If he tells you, "That was good," you believed him. When we were getting ready for a marathon, we never talked about a target time. Your training was geared toward how are you going to beat people on that course, how will you make them hurt so they quit. Bill Rodgers never thought about time. It was, as Billy would say, "Crush the other person!" And that's what Squires trained you to do was race. It wasn't about running fast, it was about trying to win the race."

Did Meyer like that approach? "Oh, hell yes! That's what running's about. So many times you hear people say, 'I ran two-something' or 'I was the first American' or 'I was happy with my time.' Yeah, but you were ninth! Get up front and race! That's what they taught us."

GBTC wins in the early 1980s were being recorded in varying distances, including in 1980 in the 5,000-meter walk (Vaitones), marathon (Palmer) and 50-mile ultra (Jim Durkin). An individual highlight for (O'Hagan) Gilligan was at the 1980 Newport Marathon when she ran a stunning sub-3:00 in a remarkable turnaround from her 1977 result of 5:05. "I was last and they had already taken down the finish line

Randy Thomas in the 1983 Boston Marathon. *Photo by Leo Kulinski Jr.*

and everybody was gone," she recalled of 1977. "A reporter for the local newspaper called me at home the next day and interviewed me on how it felt to be last. I said 'Great,' not being at all embarrassed, only so happy to have run a marathon with no training. Three years later the same reporter came up to me after I came in third in the same marathon in a time of 2:58 and asked if I could possibly be the same person who ran last in '77. I then got to thinking about how I could improve with proper training."

A bit of Grauman's Chinese Theatre–style excitement made its presence in March 1983, when a "Walkway of the Running Stars" was planted near the Eliot Lounge. In wet cement on the outdoor sidewalk, footprints were pressed by GBTC's Fleming, Hodge, Rodgers and Thomas; Boston winners Burfoot, Johnny "the Younger" Kelley and Samuelson; three-time Boston runner-up Patti (Lyons) Catalano, who would later marry Dillon; Leonard; and Ryan, a three-time top-nine Boston finisher. "It was an extreme honor, sort of like Hollywood, and I was not about to miss this opportunity," said Thomas. "I remember the temperature that day was cool, and the cement was hardening very quickly. By the time I placed my feet in the cement, I had to wiggle quite a bit to make an impression. So my footprints came out a bit on the wide side. It was an honor to participate."

In 1983–84, the ever-growing club hired coaches for the first time: multiple-marathon champion Palmer, quickly followed by original member Dick Mahoney (men's), and U.S. Olympic Trials qualifier Bob Clifford (women's), after Lane realized his real job required more of his time. To accommodate the additional range of interests, committees increased to men's road running, women's road running, track and field, social, membership, newsletter, publicity, Freedom Trail, GBTC Invitational and Women's 25K Championship. While a certain structure was lacking, according to Dick Mahoney, "I basically patterned it after what Squires had done with us with groups. I met with them once a week, gave workouts, worked with them. It was different. No offense to whoever was there, but there was not a lot of talent there. I do remember Sebastian Junger then. He was a very, very good runner. But the feeling I had at the time was that people felt because we were a well-known club that just by joining and running with us, you were automatically going to get better. And obviously that's not necessarily the case."

Interest in running was at such a peak that the city of Boston in mid-1984 had designed and marked several true-measured distances along the Charles River via Thom Gilligan, GBTC president that year. "They asked the club if someone could measure the running/cycling path around the Charles," he recalled. "I used a Jones Counter and came up with 17.8 miles from starting at the Museum of Science and running to Watertown Square and back on the Cambridge side."

At the 1983 New York City Marathon, the women's team was second with (Meade) Lavelle (2:49:45), Jean Smith (2:52:26) and Bray (2:54:44). "My goal for the 1983 NYC Marathon was to break 2:50," said (Meade) Lavelle. "Again, my training consisted of weekly hill and track workouts and the Sunday long runs. I was able to increase some of my weekly mileage to seventy-five, eighty and eighty-five with an all-time high of ninety-five miles one week. My track workout times were also improving. The weather [for New York] was fifty to fifty-three degrees and rainy—perfect weather for me when running a marathon."

In the club's relatively new category of interest, the ultra (longer than a marathon), Rick Hogan tallied up major mileage at the 1984 Lake Waramaug 50-Miler (7:11:21), Old Dominion 100-Miler (23:20) and the Ironman-distance Cape Cod Endurance Triathlon (11:48:06).

GBTC won both team titles at the 1984 National 10-Mile RRCA (Road Runners Club of America) Championships. The men's team included

In the 1984 U.S. Olympic Marathon Trials (from left) Greg Meyer (leading), Tony Sandoval (hidden), Alberto Salazar and Bill Rodgers (3). *Photo by Leo Kulinski Jr.*

Johnny Halberstadt (49:10), Clifford (52:52), Hebert (53:55), Jon Berit (54:25) and Brendan Reilly (55:55); and the women's team was made up of Jean Smith (1:04:16), Bray (1:05:08), (Meade) Lavelle (1:06:53), (O'Hagan) Gilligan (1:07:02), Hastings (1:08:42), Duckworth (1:09:40), (Fisher) Hodge (1:10:08) and Fine (1:12:58). "It was a great performance for the team!" remarked (Meade) Lavelle.

Elsewhere, Thom Gilligan won the inaugural 1984 Reykjavik Half-Marathon in Iceland (1:14:33.4) and ran a 35:10 at the "Kingly" named Bill Rodgers Cayman Islands 10K Championships. "In Boston, I was an 'also-ran.' The local competition was brutal," he said. "When I traveled, I could win races or at least be in the top ten." Fenton at the 1984 National TAC Championships was fifth in the 50K race walk (4:26:17) to qualify for the U.S. Olympic Trials, at which he came in tenth (4:46:45). And at the historic inaugural 1984 U.S. Olympic Trials women's marathon, out of nearly two hundred finishers, GBTC was represented by Lupica (99th, 2:48:56), (Meade) Lavelle (101st, 2:49:17), Bray (159th, 2:57:03) and Posie Barnett (172nd, 3:01:34).

"In 1983, I completed the Boston Marathon in 2:50:45 and finished twenty-fifth, which qualified me to run the 1984 Trials," said (Meade) Lavelle. "[The Trials] was a matter of being at the right place at the right time. I never imagined that this would be a possibility when I started running in 1977. It was an exciting and awesome experience for me that I will never forget. The event itself was well organized and a lot of fun. I pulled my left hamstring around [the] seventh or eighth mile, and the tightness increased throughout the rest of the race, causing a lot of pain; and I had to make an adjustment in my stride."

Despite a drop in membership to about 235 in 1984 and its continual discussion on whether to limit its membership, the later 1980s bore witness to high and low patches of interest and participation. GBTC saw more involvement by its members (including playing host to the Bay State Games), increased participation in its Grand Prix Race Series and a conscious effort to finally obtain a permanent office in which past trophies and awards (once found, as it was noted) could be housed. After several aborted moves, a brick-and-mortar office finally materialized in West Newton in the fall of 1984. Ironically, though, it was prescheduled to be razed in April 1985. Therefore, it was home for about half a year, thus continuing the saga. A resolution did arise, however, as the office first moved one block down the street and then to the Brighton house of the *Wingfoot Express* editor and newly hired clerk. But that would change. And numbers—both financial and member—dipped dangerously low.

In 1985, five years after his resignation letter and a dozen years from the club's inception, GBTC found itself without its guiding leader. Squires completely left the club. He was still coaching outside individuals on his own, still teaching and coaching at the new University of Massachusetts at Boston (which had taken over his Boston State College) and he was about to become an advisor for the New Balance Running Team. He felt it was time. But Squires would never be too far from GBTC, as the two are forever intrinsically connected. (In 2003, he was given an honorary lifetime membership, joining only Salazar and Rodgers, and in 2010, the GBTC Invitational Mile was permanently renamed the Bill Squires Invitational Mile.)

At the newly named Sudbury Summer Swing 10-Miler in 1985, which replaced the Women's 25K, GBTC won the team title with Audrey Leach (1:03:40), Cathy Ball (1:03:48), Jean Smith (1:05:13), (O'Hagan) Gilligan (1:06:18) and (Fisher) Hodge (1:07:32). GBTC also came in second at the 1985 NEAC Women's 20K Championships with Leach (first, 1:20:10), (Fisher) Hodge (1:23:11) and Fine (1:25:58). And a friendly yet competitive clash of titans occurred at the first annual 1985 GBTC-BAA Outdoor Dual meet at BC. Individual GBTC winners included Wallace (1,500 in 4:24.7), Mike Hagmeier (400-meter walk in 2:16), Barbara Sauer (Developmental Mile in 5:22.2), Leach (200 in 29.7, 800 in 2:25.7) and Lori Fikel (100 in 15.4).

Noted Berit, who organized the GBTC-BAA, "I started out in track and field at age thirteen in the spring of 1972 while I was in the eighth grade and still continue [to compete] to this day. The majority of the meets in high school were dual meets with team scoring, so I thought that it would be a good concept to have a dual meet with the BAA."

Despite certain successes, GBTC still struggled to regain its focus and direction from its original mission. To that end, a "body check" was administered, and the *Wingfoot Express* presented the favorable and not-so-favorable opinions and views as to where the club was headed. The past was lauded for its alumni who built the club on the foundation of hard work and determination, which produced the championships, titles and national and international recognition associated with GBTC. But it was also painfully evident that the organic development of separate groups within the club and the lack of a wider range of events, effective communication and membership involvement in some areas could potentially destroy that "brand." While no immediate remedy was offered, the concern was at least expressed.

A turnaround began to trickle in when a new group of rookies joined the club, and 93 percent of them at one point (86 of 92) actually filled out the informational questionnaire that accompanied their membership applications (putting to shame the instance when only 6 had filled out an earlier form). While the participation was encouraging, the once 400-plus-strong body was dwindling. Averaging closer to around 230 of late, membership lows of 140 (October), 110 (end of 1985) and 165 (beginning of 1986) were not encouraging. A noted problem was that the social aspect was weak, which lent to some disconnect between members. That began to change with an increase of celebrations and parties to join such longtime get-togethers as the annual post–Boston Marathon 27th Mile Party. Additions included barbecues, Red Sox games and a new club softball game and picnic.

At the 1986 NEAC indoors, the women's 4 x 800 (Leach, Sherry Roberts, Cathy Saltalamacchia and Ball) set a GBTC-record (GBTCR) 9:50.3. At the GBTC-BAA-CSU (Cambridge Sports Union) Outdoor meet, first-place GBTC times came from Roberts in the 100 (14.24) and 400 (64.2), Junger in the 880 (1:58.20) and mile (4:27), Don Callahan in the Developmental Mile (5:18) and Patricia Ezersky in the Developmental Mile (6:03). At the GBTC Invitational, Ann Marie Jankowski won the 880 (2:25.0). On the roads, John McNamara won the 1986 Boston Peace Marathon (2:28:30) and was later invited to run the 1987 Moscow Peace Marathon, where he was the first U.S. finisher.

"I was running track and cross-country in college," said *The Perfect Storm* bestselling author Junger, whose 3:56.36 still sat atop Wesleyan's 1,500 record book at the time of GBTC's fortieth anniversary. "I started running more road races after I got out of college," which included 10K times of 30:26 (Milk Run) and 30:41 (Diet Pepsi) in 1986 that resulted in his selection as that year's GBTC MVP Award recipient. "I did long runs with those guys once a week. Bob Murdock and I did a fifteen-miler once, probably averaging 5:40s. We hammered! Once in a while we'd get carried away, obviously, but we did distance training once a week, and once a week, we'd run on the track. I remember running this horrible hill work on Heartbreak Hill in a driving sleet under Dick Mahoney. Horrible! I did a lot of work on my own, but running with those guys, that really helped."

For marathons, Junger ran a 2:21:18 (1987 Pittsburgh), 2:22:46 (1985 Twin Cities) and 2:24:30 (1988 Twin Cities). "I was hoping to run an Olympic-qualifying marathon. I remember one year, I was in unbelievably good shape. I was going to qualify for Boston, and right before Boston, I came down with strep throat. I got incredibly sick. I would have run really, really fast. I never hit that level of fitness again. I did this workout where I'd run five repeat miles on the track, and then I'd have a quarter-mile recovery jog in between them; so it was a total of six miles when I crossed the finish line on the fifth repeat. I was running the total—the repeats combined with the recovery—in something like 5:00 pace. In other words, I was running 4:40s for repeat miles and 5:30 pace for the recovery quarter. I was in crazy shape. Then I got sick. I was destroyed. And then I had a cracked vertebrae. I had to stop running marathons because I hurt my back. After that, obviously, I wasn't going to the Olympics."

For GBTC, Hollywood came knocking once again, sort of, when in 1986, the club received an invitation, along with the BAA, CSU and Irish American Track Club (IATC), to hold a qualifying race to field a five-person relay team for the celebrity Jimmy Stewart Relay Marathon in California (GBTC had competed in prior years). Barb Amoscato represented GBTC on Team Boston, which came in ninth (2:31:18). Hobnobbing with the likes of actor Cesar Romero, former New England Patriot Mike Haynes of the Los Angeles Raiders and cohosts Stewart and Robert Wagner came with the distinction of being considered an elite team. And in an episode of *Spenser: For Hire*, TV's version of Robert B. Parker's Boston-based crime detective books starring Robert Urich, Hebert ran in a background scene of a faux road race during a "shootout."

Hebert recalled the experience: "A casting call went out for runners for an episode that involved Spenser trying to protect a guy who was running the marathon from would-be killers. The casting people contacted GBTC and running shops, trying to get extras to fill out the scene. I remember it being a pretty hot day, and they had us repeatedly run a scene down the street. The guy Spenser was trying to protect was an old, overweight actor they had dressed in a full velour running suit. I felt bad for the actor because it looked like he was about to die. As the scene progressed, the bad guys tried to grab the older actor, and Spenser jumped in—in a full-velour running suit—and tackled them across a table that had water cups on it. It was funny, because most of the people making up the runners were nonrunners, and when they said, "Action," they sprinted, all-out, down the street. The director apparently thought that was perfectly normal in a marathon. All we did was laugh. The cool part was, we hung around and watched them blow up a car for one scene."

On the music front, former GBTC member Barbara Brzostowski directed a video for Kozmetix frontman Lou Miami's song "Ghosts," which aired on MTV and local V-66. And on the bookshelves, a picture of Marty Traiser wearing his GBTC singlet appeared inside the oversized hardcover book *The World of Marathons* by Sandy Treadwell. The color photo was taken during

Traiser's 3:41 Bermuda Marathon. There was also a picture of Rodgers in the book from the 1981 Boston Marathon.

Regarding team titles, the men won the inaugural TAC National Half-Marathon Championships at the 1987 New Bedford Half-Marathon with Murdock (1:07:47), Clifford (1:09:51), McNamara (1:10:29), Pete Hopkins (1:11:01) and Pearson (1:11:27); and the women won the NEAC 8K Championships at the Human Race 8K.

GBTC's newsletter in 1987 saw its first set of changes in years with laser-printed crispness, new logo design (one of many), a return to half-page vertical columns, prominent masthead (which listed the seven board of directors, four officers, twelve committees, seventeen committee members, two coaches, the newsletter editor and staff of twelve), newspaper-style datelines, pictures and illustrations. As for GBTC scribes, a club list of well-known published writers includes Jon Chesto (*Boston Business Journal, Boston Herald*), Nancy Clark (nutrition books), Derderian (running books), Jim Hague

Israel Horovitz. *Courtesy Israel Horovitz.*

(sportswriter), Israel Horovitz (screenplays, scripts), Junger (bestselling books), Krise (running books), Meg Mitchell Moore (sports' writing), Ioannis Papadopoulos (Greek running magazine), Pfitzinger (training books), Rodgers (running/training books), Salazar (running/training books), Squires (running/training books) and others.

Nancy Clark started small while at GBTC. "To be honest, when I first started working as a sports nutritionist in 1980, I needed to market my business, so I started writing a monthly article with a credit line. I decided to provide information on how a sports nutritionist could help them. I also enjoyed helping GBTC members understand the power of proper fueling. My columns addressed the 'topics of the day.' I try to add enough science to be helpful, but also try to keep the info at the 'how to' level so readers leave with a nutrition nugget they can put into action."

Horovitz, the Gloucester Stage Company cofounder whose *Author! Author!* screenplay became an Al Pacino movie in 1982, noted he had been: "A fair high school sprinter. I could break eleven seconds for 100 yards. [But] I had stopped running during my twenties, smoked, did some recreational drugs, but soon started to notice what other writers were looking like. As a group, playwrights are not beauty-pageant material. For me, [GBTC] was the Red Sox of running. I couldn't imagine seriously identifying with any other team. I remember how we'd run loops around the pond with the big guns way up front. During one session, I somehow managed to stay up in the front group for four to five minutes until Tom Derderian spotted me and said, 'What the hell are you doing up here?'" It was through Derderian and his wife, Hastings, that Horovitz met his wife, the former Gillian Adams—a non-GBTC U.K. national marathon champion.

While Horovitz states he is "often overtaken by a barely moving ball of cold molasses, but that hardly seems a reason to stop," there was a time when his "self-delusion" prevailed, such as on his 1979 birthday at New York's Perrier Bloomingdales 10K that also featured a four-time Finnish Olympic gold medalist. "For some insane reason, Lasse Viren showed up on the starting line. For a certifiably insane reason, I decided to celebrate my fortieth birthday by staying with Viren." A photograph captures Viren, wearing bib number 1, incredulously looking over at comparably stratospheric bib number 4118. "Viren's staring at me in disbelief, possibly thinking he was witnessing a suicide. Viren, at this point, was world record-holder at 10K. And I'm two paces ahead of him, wearing a singlet advertising my play, *Sunday Runners in the Rain*. In the photo, Viren gives me his best WTF stare, and [then he] starts pushing the pace. I stayed with him. I had never run that fast in my life beyond 100 yards. After five miles, I had to sit down on the curb. I finished the race—walking—in 38 minutes, 34 seconds. Viren ran 29 minutes flat."

Continued Horovitz, "I love this story because it tells you much about me…but the same story tells much, much more about our sport, about road racing. In road racing, the greats share the road with the near-greats and not-so-greats. We all cover the same distance, and we all do our level best. And, at the end of the race, self-respect arrives in equal doses for all. It's a marvelous, primitive sport."

At the rainy 1979 Perrier Bloomingdales 10K in New York, temporary leader Israel Horovitz (4118) of GBTC ignores the stare from two-time 10,000-meter Olympic gold medalist Lasse Viren of Finland (1). *Courtesy Israel Horovitz.*

On a down note, the Freedom Trail—won by such well-known names as Bickford, Steve Jones, Meyer, Rodgers, Salazar and Thomas—did not run. Despite assistance from the mayor's office, it succumbed to a lack of sponsorship. Although GBTC's treasury was finally beginning to show some steady growth, and it was decided not to empty it for the race, funds fell dangerously low again, low enough in 1988 that both the men's and women's coaches departed when faced with reduced salaries (Berit for the men and Kevin Hicks for the women stepped up in the interim). "I remember very strongly that I wanted to coach," recalled Berit, who was second in the 3,000-meter steeplechase at the 1989 TAC National Masters Championships. "I wanted to make sure that everyone's needs were met, so I sat down with everyone to get their feedback. For instance, one individual wanted to sprint rather than doing the distances. He had assumed that the club was all about distance running, so he just went along for the ride until I took over the coaching reins."

A relatively new board greeted 1988 with much to repair, improve and set in motion (in 1987, the annual membership fee had its first increase—up five dollars to twenty-five and first-time membership to thirty). On several positive notes, the GBTC Grand Prix added a cross-country event; a larger contingent of members attended the annual meeting; the treasury was reported to have increased nearly 240 percent from the previous year; and it was pointed out that GBTC and the *Wingfoot Express* gained publicity and mention in various media, including *Boston Running News*, *City Sports*, *Running Times* and *Runner's World* magazines, as well as *Runner's Digest*, Toni Reavis's successful radio show. "It was a good local track club, but then you started realizing it when Bill won [Rabat]—that was a big thing. Then Boston, and it all took off," Reavis recalled. "The whole thing was an organic growth. And we knew it as we lived it, that this was something special. I remember [during the 1979 Boston Marathon] Jason Kehoe turned to me and said, 'Toni, these are the good ol' days.' We reveled in it, we celebrated it constantly, but never took it for granted. "

Also, there was an upswing in masters activities (since, naturally, early members were beginning to enter this new territory), especially for women. "The women of GBTC that started running in the late 1970s and grew up to be masters and seniors were some of the greatest people to know and run with," stated Fine. "People came and went, and now most of us aren't still running with the club. But [in] the 1980s and 1990s as we became masters and then seniors, we were an incredibly cohesive group." In GBTC's fifteenth year, the women's master's team won the 1988 NEAC 30K Championship title with Sauer (first, 2:12:02), Duckworth (2:17:04), (O'Hagan) Gilligan (2:18:55) and Fine (2:25:55); and the 1988 NEAC 10-Mile Championship with Sauer (1:08:20), Duckworth (1:09:58) and Fine (1:13:27).

Lois Brommer Duquette (who married GBTC's Ralph Duquette) recalled that while women in races was becoming the norm and the vast majority of people accepting, there were still pockets of resentment: "I remember a race where some big guy was upset that I passed him. This was the late 1980s, and some guys still could not handle being beat by a woman. Ironically, as I mentioned, he was big, and he did not look like someone who could not have been beaten by a woman before. When I passed him, he started yelling at me, so I ran even faster. There was no way I was going to let that guy catch me on the course. At the finish, he was yelling at my husband and me. He said I did something when I passed him. I have no idea what. I think he was upset that I was faster than him."

(O'Hagan) Gilligan won the 1988 Bermuda Marathon (3:19) with her club training. It had been en route to the 1980 edition of the British Isles race when she met future husband Thom Gilligan. She proceeded to follow his instruction, which eventually led her to the structured coaching of Newman and Clifford.

"Thom taught me that you do not necessarily need athletic prowess to succeed in sports, but rather discipline and a lot of hard work," she said. "[Then with] Larry and a great group of highly motivated gals, [and with Clifford], he and Larry had different styles, but both taught us much in regards to discipline which has followed me my whole life and has always been a code to live by."

Also in 1988, Junger won the wintertime Hyannis Half-Marathon (CR 1:09:43). "I was running by myself on that. I generally just ran as hard as I could. I was pretty determined," noted Junger, who also recalled another cold run. "I remember a thirteen-miler with Bob [Murdock]. It was brutally cold—teens, single digits—really windy, nighttime in Watertown. We headed out the door and turned into this blast of arctic wind, and he shouts in my ear, 'It's not the heat, it's the humidity,'" Junger laughs. "The company helps."

After fifteen years in Cape Cod, the eight-leg, 65.1-mile Plymouth to Provincetown Relay moved up north to the New Hampshire Gunstock ski area as the newly christened Lake Winnipesaukee Relay. The GBTC open women's team (Lynn Cornelius, Marianne DiMascio, Julie Donohoe Hussey, Duckworth, Janet McGill, Claire McManus, Karen Rattray and Jean Smith) was third. And the winners of the eight-contest GBTC Grand Prix race series stayed in-house, literally, with the titles won by husband and wife Chris Hussey and Donohoe Hussey.

The decade closed with a serious look at increasing the club's road-race schedule in an effort to add to its treasury and whether to hold new monthly meetings at the Eliot to continue the dialogue on various matters in the hopes that a greater social setting may be more inviting for members. Also, Berit (men's) and Ralph Duquette (women's) were hired as coaches. And when Berit moved from interim to hired coach, he still maintained his personal approach. "I made sure that I talked with everyone regardless of ability level. For some, the fact that I knew their name was worth the price of admission. After the Boston Marathon one particular year, I called up everyone to make sure that they were okay. One individual thought this to be a great gesture on my part and always remembered it years later. My goals for the club were to increase participation in cross-country and track and field. There were several athletes who I introduced to these two disciplines."

Brommer Duquette recognized the expert coaching the women received. "I am going to come across as biased, but I think Ralph did a good job of providing workouts that could help runners of all abilities. He also tried very hard to keep the club from becoming only a social running club and to continue its tradition of developing competitive runners as well. At the time, there was a lot of resistance by some members to the efforts to remain competitive."

Chapter Three

1990–1999

This was a time when it was rare to hear talk of a member aiming for an Olympic Trials qualification, national title or major-marathon win. The 1990s slipped through with but a handful of local and regional cross-country and track titles and an occasional dip in the national pool. However, GBTC did open its third decade with the continuation of top scores from the women's teams and a welcomed rekindled interest in track.

At the Lake Winnipesaukee Relay, the women's masters team was unstoppable for half the decade. Some of the legs throughout the years were run by Joan Bernard, Nancy Clark, Duckworth, Fine, (O'Hagan) Gilligan, Kay McDonald, Sandy Miller, Joanne Morris, Barbara Nelson, Claudia Patrick, Judy Pruitt, Judy Romvos, Sauer and Jean Smith. Also victorious at the 1991 Lake Winnie was the mixed team of Domenic Parrotta, Rachel Shanor, Rattray, Bill Newsham, Brommer Duquette, John Nickerson, Cornelius and Hussey. And at the 1993 Stu's 30K, GBTC won the women's masters title with Duckworth, Romvos and Fine.

"We had a number of strong runners," noted Brommer Duquette. "The one [Winnipesaukee] I really remember, we were behind when I got the baton. I think my leg was all uphill to the finish—at least it felt that way—at a ski resort. I was a pretty strong hill runner at the time and so that worked in my favor, and I was able to pass the other team. It was very fun to be part of the winning team." Added Nancy Clark, "The friends with whom you run will be your friends forever. I'm grateful for how GBTC enriched both my personal and professional life and provided experiences that added to my knowledge about nutrition in action." Kay McDonald also remembered the

At the Lake Winnipesaukee Relay. *Front row, from left*: Erin (Cullinane) Kandamar, Melinda (Casey), Doane, Debbie Brendemuehl, Donna Pauler; *back row*: Mike Wyatt, Sean Mullan, Mark Tuttle, Mark Hickman. *Courtesy Erin (Cullinane) Kandamar.*

camaraderie of other races, including a Tufts Health Plan 10K highlight, in which "I came in 97th. Very cool running in the front with fewer women and finishing the race at the front when I was so used to running the Tufts 10K in the pack with thousands of other women all around me."

Individual wins were turned in throughout the '90s, including at the 1992 NEAC Championships at Brown's Alden Invitational with Eamonn Browne (mile), and Lisa Conboy, Wendy Cipelle, Shanor and Gill (4 x 800). At the 1992 NEAC All-Comers, Serge Prepetit won the 100. At the 1993 NEAC, John McGuirl, Prepetit, Claudio Badea and Pershing Reid (4 x 100) won. At the 1995 USATF/GBTC Wednesday Night Challenge—the inaugural four-part mini-meet series of competitions in the 100, 800, mile and long jump that culminated at the Eleventh Annual GBTC Invitational Relays—wins came from Kevin Russell (100 tie), Newsham (mile), Donohoe Hussey (mile). At the 1996 USATF-NE, Newsham won the mile. At the 1996 USATF-NE Open-Master's

Championship, Sandy Miller took the 800; also in 1996, at the Bay State Games, Jim Pawlicki won the 3,000-meter steeplechase and the 5,000. At the 1999 New England Track Championships, Johann Jack took first in the 100 and 200; and in the 1999 USATF-NE indoors at Alden, which served as the USATF-NE Men's Indoor Track Championship, wins came from Deon Barrett (5,000), John Blouin, Terry O'Neill, Ben Pease, Mark Reeder (men's DMR), Christina Manolatou, Maura Mahoney, Maria Sun, Livvy Williams (women's DMR), Moeen Cheema (TJ) and Julie Spolidoro (3,000). Also, at the 1999 USATF-NE at the New England Limited Indoor Track

GBTC hurdler logo for twentieth anniversary in 1993. *Courtesy GBTC.*

Meet, Spolidoro won the mile. For New England track team titles, GBTC won the 1998 and 1999 men's indoors.

In addition, multiple track wins of note came from Andrew Parker in the 400 at the 1992 Dartmouth Relays, Dartmouth Invitational, and Metrowest Twilight; Reid in the 55 (undefeated 1992–93 indoors) and 200 (only one loss); Wayne Fisher in 1995 in the 55 (Brown's All-Comers #2), 100 (USATF-NE Master's), 200 (USATF-NE Master's), 400 (Brown), LJ (Brown, USATF-NE Open-Master's); and Amory Rowe Salem, who in only her second mile for GBTC, won the 1997 Norm Levine Classic Indoor Track Meet in a MR 5:20.53 to remain undefeated. Later in the year, she scored the sudden death–winning goal at the Lacrosse World Cup Championships in Japan to defend the title for the United States.

"Yes, 1997 was a great year!" she exclaimed and continued: "But I was living a sort of schizophrenic athletic life at that point. I was deeply immersed in the tryout process for the U.S. World Cup Team, and at the same time, I was falling in love with the completely new and different sport of running. Happily, one fueled the other. All due credit to Bill Durette here, as he kept my head on straight. The first few races I did—all mile races—he told me I had to be in last place at the halfway point, and then I could do whatever I wanted with 800 meters to go. I was notching some truly silly negative splits, but I was also just learning how to run on a track—and an indoor track at that—how to be patient, how to pass, etc. It was all quite new and exciting."

Rowe Salem's score over Australia secured the fourth lacrosse championship title to date for the United States. "At that point, I had become so enamored of running that I would get up early and run though the city. It was a beautiful time of day and a beautiful way to see the city and gain the perspective needed during an otherwise stressful time. Looking back, that time in Japan laid the groundwork for my appreciation of running as something other than raw competition; it was a way to see and interact with a new environment as well as an opportunity to take a few deep breaths to ground oneself."

In cross-country, the women won back-to-back USATF-NE titles (1993–94) and the men were champions in 1995. Also, at the Lynn Woods Cross-Country 10-Mile Relay, the women won three consecutive team titles in 1997 (Rowe Salem, Joanna Veltri, Joyce Dendy and Jennifer Rapaport), 1998 (Susan Wiseman, Sue Bergh, Erin [Cullinane] Kandamar and Kerry O'Donovan), 1999 (Manolatou, Livvy Williams, Maura McDonald and Elaine Abeguile). The men won back-to-back titles in 1997 (Kifle Alemu, Blouin, Pawlicki and Jesse Darley) and 1998 (Darley, Barrett, Jim Reardon and Blouin). The women also repeated team wins at the Noble and Greenough Cross-Country 5K in 1997 (Veltri, Rapaport and Donohoe Hussey) and 1998 (Shawna Nehiley, Payal Parekh and Hastings). And with three straight CRs, Donohoe Hussey won the Conservation 2.5-Mile Cross-Country Series #6 (16:15), #7 (15:30) and #8 (15:27).

Other harrier success came at the 1995 Reebok USATF-NE championships, where the men won the team title; the 1997 Yankee Runner 5K, won by Darley; the 1997 New England Grand Prix Race Series, won by the GBTC women; the 1999 Home Depot Invitational 8K, with five of the top ten spots from Glen Mays (fourth), Barrett (fifth), Mark Tompkins (eighth), Ethan Crain (ninth) and Darley (tenth); and the 1999 USATF nationals, which marked the first time in club history with both the men's and women's teams competing. GBTC also captured the 1998 USATF-NE Grand Prix titles when, in the final event of the series, the men came in fourth and the women sixth at the New Englands.

Also of special note, GBTC's Rosemary Phelan in 1990, in one span of nearly two dozen races, won thirteen age-group awards and came in second or third in eight others and, in 1991, continued her reign, which also included top veteran-category honors at the 1991 Hyannis Sprint Triathlon, where she joined fellow club member Lauri Gavenda, who also won her age group.

Ann King recalled the fun times GBTC had at the 185-mile, 17-leg Cabot Trail Relay Race in Canada in 1993 (sixth) and 1994 (third) with teams consisting of Bruce Bond, Cipelle, King, McManus, Newsham and Dick Nickerson, as well as Tom Richardson on the multiclub Team Massachusetts U.S.A. One year, "Tom chose a late-night leg on chance he might see the aurora borealis. Instead, there was a storm with gale-force winds, driving rain and hail! Another memory was [us] desperately looking to see a moose. All day and all night we were looking, looking. Meanwhile, Claire was sleeping in the van. Sleeping, sleeping, until one moment she sat up, and *she* saw a moose! None of the rest of us did then or anytime the whole trip." And after the race, "We all looked forward to the lobster dinner at the end, not realizing that in Nova Scotia, they eat their lobster cold! They were the nicest, friendliest people we ever met, however."

Brommer Duquette, who won the famous literary James Joyce Ramble 10K in 1991, did have her sights set on qualifying for the U.S. Olympic Trials at the Dallas White Rock Marathon. But while her 2:58:16 landed her as the fourth-place woman at the 1991 42K, it missed the required standard mark. "I found the team long runs helpful to help build up the mileage in a pleasant way, and I really enjoyed running in the Grand Prix races for the team," she said. "The Dallas Marathon was tough. I had just started working as a lawyer in a big firm, and I was trying to get an Olympic Trials qualifying time; [and] the two didn't necessarily go together. I signed up for Dallas as a last attempt before winter weather set in. Unfortunately, that weekend in Dallas, it was unusually cold, windy and raining. It was something like thirty-six and rain and windy all around a lake we ran. So, conditions were pretty brutal."

The pavement also was a place for success with many red-singlet road-race victories. Darley won the 1999 Jones-Town & Country 10-Miler—founded in 1975 by Derderian—which served as the USATF-NE Grand Prix 10-Mile Championship. The 1997 USATF-NE Road Race Grand Prix Series, which consisted of seven races from 5K to the marathon, featured Bond, Karen Crouse, Tom Guerrini, Hubert "Hugh" Jessup, Jim O'Leary, Michelle Parks and Pawlicki as GBTCers who competed in every event. And at the three-state 1998 Eastern States 20-Miler, it was a shootout between Darley (first, 1:51:40) and Pawlicki (second, 1:51:44). Over three days in the fall of 1997, Lisa Frank, Kristin Mattocks, Parks and Jean Smith participated in the annual Boston to New York AIDS Ride 3, a 250-mile fundraising bike trek. Bond, incidentally, started weekly Sunday long runs in the pristine Walden Woods in Concord, a GBTC practice that still continues.

"[After Eastern States] I was still feeling decent, so I decided to jump over a barrier at the finish-line chute," recalled Pawlicki. "I nearly fell over, not

Hubert "Hugh" Jessup in the 2002 Boston Marathon. *Photo by Frank Monkiewicz.*

anticipating what my legs would feel like after twenty miles. My legs just about cramped up. I made a note not to goof off after any long distance races like that again."

As the club approached its twentieth anniversary in 1993, membership leveled at just over one hundred; the forever-tenuous treasury forced an increase in membership dues to thirty-five dollars; and a renewed focus was directed toward keeping the club out of the red (other than the GBTC singlet). There was also an effort to simplify matters, as annual terms of membership would run from the month a person joined instead of automatically from October to October (it would eventually change to a calendar year) and a reduction of committees but the addition of captains was implemented. Social gatherings also were invigorated with the inclusion of golf outings, ski trips, a weekend running camp and even interest in Ultimate Frisbee.

Perhaps the platinum anniversary was a reawakening for the club, because the mid-1990s was also when the embryonic stages of a resurgence and refocus began. Berit received his TAC Level 1 certification by the sport's national governing body, which instituted a number of standardized levels of accreditation through various programs on the disciplines of running and track and field. "In 1993, the TAC certification became available in the Boston area, so I took advantage of it," he pointed out. "The club was starting to get more well-rounded again as far as disciplines were concerned instead of just being a club for distance runners."

At the Eliot, the ten-year-old "Walkway of the Running Stars" sidewalk of footprints was torn up in 1993 as part of pedestrian city construction. When the dust settled, it was reassembled with a new cast of stars, which included GBTC's Hodge, Rodgers and Squires; Boston Marathon champions Johnny "the Elder" Kelley and Geoff Smith; Leonard; and Jennings. Also, on a festive note, the club's twentieth was celebrated at a GBTC-sponsored Heart and Sole Road Race postrace bash that featured hundreds of former and current members, some of whom over the years had met their eventual spouses at the club. Honored guests at the gala included original members Elliot, Dick Mahoney, Pfrangle, Sevene and Squires and special guests Concannon, Grilk, Hodge, Meyer, Newman, Rodgers and many others.

And speaking of Squires—who as a Notre Dame miler had once maneuvered through tornado winds and tumbling hurdles during a track meet that was soon cancelled due to the storm—Durette in the spring of 1994 attempted to equal the master when, while coaching a weekday workout, he was reportedly struck by lightning. Other than a suddenly heated top of the noggin, he fortunately escaped relatively unscathed.

A new era began in 1994, when GBTC hired Derderian, a 2:19:04 marathoner (1975 Boston) whose primary focus was men's distance. The forty-five-year-old had run for GBTC (1978–84) because it "was the only game in town. Everyone who was aspiring was in Greater Boston. Unlike now, there was no money on the table. You weren't beating someone at a race in order to get a pay day, [nor] were you trying to go to a race where there was no one in order to win and get some money. In fact, it was looked at as a rather cowardly thing to do to not go to the best race, not go to where the best competition was." That year also marked the release of Derderian's conclusive *Boston Marathon: The History of the World's Premier Running Event*, for which he won the 1995 RRCA Journalistic Excellence Award; and in 1996, the book was updated and reissued as a Centennial Race Edition called *Boston Marathon: The First Century of the World's Premier Running Event.*

Prior to Derderian as coach, recent training consisted of scheduled long runs and evening workouts. While the basis for this system, to an extent, dated back to the club's beginning, members around this time would show up and off they went. It lacked hard-lined goals and structure. In the early days, Squires had developed a more precise goal-oriented, three-group program, in which separate groups were designed toward talent- and goal-based workouts. "It's just too easy to say we're going every Tuesday night and go to this track and do this workout, and with workouts not tailored for the specific athletes, like, here's a workout of 3 x 1200 and no matter what you're training for, that's what you're running," noted Doyle. "That's not what we did. We had different groups depending on [talent, goals, etc.]."

Derderian, having experienced Squires's program as well as others throughout his career, noticed that "it had become sort of a jogging club—not exactly, but pretty close to that—where people would go to the once-a-week workouts and go through the motions of training and then go for pizza and beer. It'd become a health/fitness organization rather than an organization dedicated to winning. So what I did was go back to the Squires kind of idea where he wanted to win every national championship." Derderian emphasized to his new troops that he wanted GBTC to "show up at races as a team and compete as a team and make an impact as a whole group, and that we would aim toward the New England Grand Prix races and organize our team in that direction."

A return to that communal spirit, that sense of belonging and sharing, in practice and for out-of-state competitions, was vital for Derderian to reestablish. "[Workouts] are not a school assignment where they say, 'I'll make it up another day. I'll do it tomorrow.' That's what doesn't work. You build an emotional commitment because other people are suffering, or suffering and pretending not to be suffering. Getting the club organized to raise the money to go to these places is another thing that brings people together. It's not easy to do that."

The late 1990s also witnessed change to the *Wingfoot Express* and the club's state-of-the-art website, which was the fruit of the expert labor of GBTC's Mark Tuttle. In addition to the new coaching design for its 165 members, the newsletter in 1995 also reflected a new look with what was explained as access to nouveau techno called the "Internet," "World Wide Web" and "electronic mail," as means for information and communication. In fact, the *Wingfoot* became available electronically on the website, an online store was created to serve its membership (which peaked at about 200 after an average of 150–175 in the latter years) and a GBTC Hotline phone number was created. And during this transition into the future, Michael Turmala became the first two-term club president since John Heffernan (1986–87).

Russell and Veltri set several point-scoring records in accordance with the IAAF, which calculates point values. At the 1998 GBTC Invitational Relays, Russell scored 970 points with his 48.36 in the 400 and Veltri 912 points with her 5:02.17 in the mile. Veltri also twice broke her own record with 921 points at the 1998 BU Terrier Classic via her 10:09.13 in the 3,000, and then again with 925 points at the New England indoors with her 17:37.41 in the 5,000.

GBTC's silver anniversary in 1998 was celebrated with an evening gathering at the Mount Auburn Club in Watertown, where Squires regaled the masses with tales of yore.

Chapter Four

2000–2009

The new century continued the trend of consistent prominence, especially with New England championships. Out of a possible combined forty men and women New England track team titles, GBTC won all but three. The men's team swept the decade with the indoor and outdoor titles, and the women won the indoors from 2001 to 2009 and the outdoors from 2001 to 2003 and from 2005 to 2009. The men also won the USATF East Club Regional Championship in 2002–03 and 2007 and the women in 2003 and 2005–08.

In 2001, Jack set numerous GBTCRs—some of which, as of the club's fortieth, remain in the top five in the 55, 100, 200 and 4 x 100 lists. "I had a lot to prove in 2001," he said, which included his 100 (10.35) and 200 (21.38) at Duke. "[The 100] was a huge surprise. The competition reminded me of David and Goliath—I was so small compared to the other diesel machines! The only thing I could remember was repeating to myself, 'Run faster, faster, faster.' [For the 200] I was going to this meet for the first time as a GBTC [member], and I was in the zone. I focused on running the turns hard and slingshotting out of the 150-mark and coasting for 80 meters and hanging in for dear life if I had anything left in me! And guess what? The plan worked."

Stanley Egbor had a tremendous 2003 with wins at the USATF East Regional Championship 100 (10.31) and 200 (20.66) and the GBTC Invitational 60 (6.73), marks which still top GBTC in its fortieth year. "[It] was the best and most painful year in my running career. I came into the season after a difficult loss at the last meet of the previous season, and I was determined not only to avenge—for lack of a better word—that loss but also to have a breakout season. Some of the goals I set were to own the club records in the 60, 100 and 200. I knew the previous record holder, and I admired him back then." The USATF 100 and 200 was also satisfying because of the competition. "An added benefit was that I beat the guy who beat me the previous year, the guy who was responsible for me coming into this season with the focus I had. It felt so, so, so good. And he knew it, too. He knew I was coming for him."

At the USATF National Club Track and Field Team Championships, GBTC won the women's title in 2002, 2006 and 2009, the men's in 2002 and the combined title in 2002 and 2005. Several athletes also set a number of MRs for their national titles:

2005: Jennifer Lee, Sloan Siegrist, Jane Cullina and Laura Hayden (women's 4 x 800).

2006: Kelly Powell, Lee, Caroline Occean and Anna Willard (women's 4 x 800).

2009: Samyr Laine (TJ) and Ayanna Alexander (TJ).

Regarding the 2006 nationals at Mt. San Antonio College, Willard recalled, "I had a great time with the GBTC at the national meet at Mt. SAC, California. The 4 x 800 has always been an event close to my heart, as track and field is typically an individual sport. I have fond memories of my teammates cheering me on and fueling me to equal my 800-meter PR at the time so that GBTC could be elevated to the win." The 2008 U.S. Olympian also known for her splashes of colorful hair noted, "In 2006, my hair was somewhat tame compared to how it is colored now. I had a bright blonde streak in the front."

Additionally, GBTC wins for national champion status came from several athletes:

2001: Joe Welch (hammer).

2002: Joan Bohlke (800); Michelle Carrancho (TJ); Sarah Lawson, Keely Subin, Kourtney Trainor and Bohlke (4 x 400).

2003: Marzuki Stevens (3,000-meter steeplechase), Ulrike Gradhand (400-meter hurdles).

2004: Dan Olson (HJ); Catherine Regan, Lawson, Nastaran Shams, Siegrist (DMR).

2005: Olson (HJ); Sean Furey (javelin); Sherita Williams (TJ); Natalie Grant (hammer); Kateema Riettie (javelin); Sara O'Brien, Caroline Finlay, Shams, Occean (sprint medley).

The GBTC team on the fabled Icahn Stadium field in New York after the 2009 USATF National Club Track and Field Championship, where they won the women's title, grabbed fourth in the men's and took second in the combined. *GreaterSnap photo courtesy GBTC.*

At the 2009 BAA Invitational Mile, Anna Willard in the lead, ahead of Shalane Flanagan and Amy Mortimer. *Photo by Paul C. Clerici.*

2006: Furey (javelin); Aaron Binkley, Josh Seeherman, Andie Colon, Joseph Otto (4 x 800); Willard (1,500); Riettie (SP, javelin).

2007: Andrew Hall (javelin).

2008: Hector Cotto (110-meter hurdles), Laine (TJ), Tessa Clare (HJ).

2009: Jennifer Harlow (HJ), Joeane Jadotte (SP, discus).

Willard followed her 2006 USATF relay and 1,500 titles with national and international track success, noting of GBTC, "It was a great experience, one that helped catapult me into the professional track and field circuit. The DMR and the 4 x 800 are more memorable to me because it was a joyous moment shared with new teammates. I joined the GBTC in the summer of 2006 because I hail from the Northeast and was looking for some more competitive opportunities through the summer after my collegiate season had ended at Brown University."

The women's DMR team of Lee, Sara O'Brien, Occean and Allison McCabe set a GBTCR at the 2008 AT&T U.S.A. Indoor Track and Field Championships (11:41.91). Recalls the anchor, "We all had good races, which is unusual that everyone has a good day on the same day. Relays are my favorite, and I'm glad that as a postcollegiate runner I can still take part in these events."

At the USATF National Master's Indoor Track and Field Championships, many GBTC age-group wins were recorded:

2001: Vic Radzevich (pole vault [PV]), Steve Keyes (LJ), Art Henson (HJ), James Bateman, Jon Ellis, Brian Moore, Chris Simpson (4 x 400), Ellis, Bateman, Stephen Putnam, Simpson (4 x 800).

2003: Deke Conkin (LJ).

2004: Christy Bonstelle (mile, 3,000.)

2005: Colin McArdle (mile, 3,000).

2006: Lawson (60).

2007: Dave Cahill (800), men's 4 x 400.

2008: Cahill (800).

2009: Jason Hewitt (800), Richard Harrison (SP).

Most impressive was the consistency with which GBTC displayed its wins, whether by individuals or various teams. So much so that USATF-NE took notice and named the entire team(s) as its Athlete(s) of the Month for July 2006 in recognition of its numerous top individual and team results, including three team titles.

Historically at the USATF National Cross-Country Championships, GBTC has not fared well. The best men's finish was eleventh in 1999 and the best women's, tenth in 2002. But as Squires always preached, "It's worth mixing it up to get your nose bled" against better competition. "I'll clue ya," he directs, "that's how you learn." Derderian agrees, stating, "I decided that the club should compete in cross-country; try to win the USATF-NE championships in track, indoors and outdoors; have women's teams; go to the club nationals in cross-country and track and field."

On the roads this decade, teams and individuals took likings to several annual events. Within a span of twenty-three days in 2000 alone Mays won the Great Stew Chase 15K, Martha's Vineyard 20-Miler, Cape Cod Marathon. Ben Nephew won the 2000–02 Merrimack River Trail Run 10-Miler and the twelve-mile 7 Sisters Trail Race (2001, 2005). Other multiple-year wins included the Stew Chase (2008 David Bedoya, 2001 Lynn Johnson), Cape Cod Marathon relay (2005 open men's team, 2005–06 open women's team and 2006 mixed team), Hyannis Half-Marathon (2008 Andrew Womack, 2003 Jessica Blake, 2005–06 Johnson, 2002–06 men's open relay, 2004–06 and 2008 women's open relay and 2005 men's masters relay), Stu's 30K (2004 J.R. Cruz, 2004 Blake and 2005 Maegan Chaggaris), Eastern States 20-Miler (2004 Kit Wells, 2008 Bedoya and 2008 Tara [Vance] Womack) and the accompanying half-marathon (2008 Johnson).

Several members of GBTC have gone to compete in international competitions. Geraldine Pillay represented South Africa at the African Championships (2002–08), IAAF World Indoor Track Championships (2003–07), Olympics (2004) and the Commonwealth Games (2006) as a six-time medalist. For Guam, Siegrist won silver at the 2003 South Pacific Games and competed in the 2004 IAAF World Indoor Track Championships and 2004 Olympics. Representing Jamaica, Riettie won bronze at the 2008 Central American and Caribbean Championships (CACC). For Puerto Rico, Cotto medaled at the 2008 CACC. For Greece, Papadopoulos was fourteenth out of thirty-three at the 2009 Greek National Championship 5K. For Trinidad and Tobago, Alexander won gold at the 2007 North American CACC and bronze at the 2008 CACC while Jack competed in the European International Circuit. For Nigeria, Egbor was fourth in the 200 at the 2003 Adidas Boston Indoor Games.

Egbor commented, "I worked hard coming into the [2003] season—added weightlifting and pretty much decided I would compare myself to world-class athletes. That thought-process actually helped me; it gave me a mental edge going into every meet against the other athletes." But while competing to represent Nigeria, Egbor injured his quadriceps in the 100. "At about 80 meters I was in a tough battle with this other guy, and I went to what my college coach called 'another gear.' But this time, my quad muscle just popped. I only finished that race on sheer momentum."

Papadopoulos, to prepare for the Greek race, relied on his GBTC coach prior to his trip. "I remember preparing for the 5K race one week before in Boston with Tom Derderian timing my splits [on] a rainy afternoon. I had to do 5 x 1,000 meters in 2:58–3:00. It felt tough at the time. The weather conditions in Thessaloniki, the second largest Greek city, were bad. Even at 8:00 p.m., the humidity was close to 90 percent and the temperature was stuck in the hundreds. I raced wearing the GBTC singlet but representing the track team of [my] hometown, Kilkis. I managed to finish in 15:43. It was a race that could have gone better for me. [But] all the training and mileage I did in Boston have been a valuable asset that helped me improve when I came back to Greece in 2010." He was sixth at the 2011 Greek Marathon Championships, seventh at the 2011 Greek 10K Championships and second at the 2012 Balkan Marathon Championships while representing his homeland (PR 2:29:47).

Jack, a holder of multiple New England records who roomed with GBTC's David Callum at BU, always maintained lofty goals. "I was eager to compete at the world-class level to represent either my home country of Trinidad and Tobago or the United States in the European Preseason International Circuit, whichever would support my endeavor. I had logged all my workouts from 1994–2006, and I remember going over it with Dave, looking at how each year I was getting faster and faster. It was cool to see that every meet that I started out slow, [and] by the end of the spring season, I was on the right track."

Individual honors this decade included Nephew named 2000 Trail Runner of the Year by *New England Runner* magazine and Sherita Williams named USATF-NE Athlete of the Month for January, when she set the GBTCR, MR and field house record in the triple jump (PR 44-0.75) at the 2006 GBTC Invitational. In 2002, the National Distance Running Hall of Fame and Nike honored Squires with the prestigious Bill Bowerman Coaching Award. Two years later, Squires joined his good friend Arthur Lydiard, the New Zealand coaching legend, at a speaking engagement Derderian organized for the Kiwi great at Regis College. Lydiard, who died one month later, had always embraced Squires, an advisory staff member of the Lydiard Foundation. And in 2003, in addition to its yearly slate of club awards, the first GBTC Recognition Award was presented to stalwart member and contributor Bob

At Nike headquarters in Oregon in 2001. *From left*: Bill Squires, Mark Duggan, John "Jocko" Connolly (behind Michael Johnson statue), Scott Graham, Fred Doyle, Kirk Pfrangle. *Courtesy Fred Doyle.*

Club president Doug Burdi (left) presents Bob Ward with the first GBTC Recognition Award in 2003. *Courtesy GBTC.*

Ward, a marathoner whose strength was evident through his remarkable recovery from brain surgery, open-heart surgery and coma.

The early 2000s also was a time of internal review and change, as GBTC updated its mission statement and renewed its nonprofit status as a tax-exempt 501(c)(3) organization. In 2005, in response to the loss of sponsorship revenue, advertising began to appear on its website as well as in the (online, paper, e-mailed and newfangled "portable document folder" PDF) pages of the *Wingfoot Express*. And Gary Snyder became the longest-serving president to date with five consecutive years of service from 1998 to 2002. "When I was elected GBTC president, the club's resources was about $1,500, and membership was declining," he noted. "At the time, the club was sponsoring several longtime events that were losing money. I was the region CFO at a large corporation and helped the [GBTC board] institute a simple budget process and some financial responsibility. [Also], GBTC won the track and field club championships, which was a big deal at the time. The [board] had a big discussion to go or not, as it was going to be very expensive. But we won enough money to even have a nice surplus."

Throughout this decade, the club's involvement in its regional governing body grew to the point where members were consistently elected to office in its USATF-NE branch. It started in 1998 with Jim O'Brien (treasurer) and Veltri (athlete representative) and continued over the next few years:

2001: Simpson (athlete representative).

2002: Snyder (president), Jim O'Brien (treasurer), Terry O'Neill (track and field chairperson), Simpson (athlete representative).

2003: (Cullinane) Kandamar (women's long distance chairperson).

2004: Snyder (president).

2006: Callum, who replaced Cahill (track and field chairman), Newsham (cross-country chairman), Lawson (athlete representative), Seeherman (athlete representative).

Snyder was also voted as the USATF Master's Track and Field chairman in 2006. In addition, GBTC was selected as one of the initial clubs in the inaugural group of USATF's Elite Development Club Program, which awarded the designation to nineteen clubs for the 2008 Olympics. "Being elected president was recognition of the reputation of GBTC in New England," Snyder acknowledged. "The USATF membership was looking to our club for leadership in many ways."

GBTC's victorious women's team at the 2004 Boston Marathon. *From left*: coach Tom Derderian, Laura Hayden, Margaret Bradley, Jessica Blake. New England Runner *photo by Bob Fitzgerald.*

At the 2004 Boston Marathon, GBTC won the women's team title with Blake, Margaret Bradley and Hayden. "We were pretty surprised to hear that we had won the team title," recalled Hayden, who marveled at the awards ceremony. "We were standing among some of the fastest runners in the world, and I was just floored at how simple and understated the atmosphere was, in a really good way. The vibe was clearly to celebrate runners as people, not runners as superstars." And at the 2008 Boston Marathon, Papadopoulos, on his way to a 2:47, also encountered greatness. "I was on route for a new PR when I had a really bad hamstring cramp on Beacon Street. I was ready to collapse when a man came out from the crowd and held me. He told me that the race was over for me. He thought I was dehydrated. I asked him to stretch my leg and help me get back on my feet. He did help and then he asked if I knew who he was. Frank Shorter was his name. A former U.S. Olympic medalist was humble enough to help an unknown runner like me. I thanked him and finished."

Hollywood (sort of) once again came knocking at GBTC, when in July 2005, Paula Donovan was tapped to become part of the Syfy Channel cable reality show *Ghost Hunters*, which followed a group of, well, ghost hunters from the Rhode Island–based The Atlantic Paranormal Society (TAPS). And in January 2006, Eric Tucker appeared in a national Nike television commercial.

Regarding GBTC-connected, running-related books, Derderian in 2003 added to his résumé *The Boston Marathon: A Century of Blood, Sweat, and Cheers*, an expanded version of the 1996 accordion-style promotional book for the John Hancock Mutual Life Insurance Company called *Boston Marathon: 100 Years of Blood, Sweat, and Cheers*. Featured in both editions were photographs and descriptions of several GBTC athletes, including Clifford, Crouse, John Delany, Duckworth, Fine, Hall, Jessup, Rania Matar, Meyer, Rodgers, Salazar and Squires. In 2009, the year after GBTC's thirty-fifth anniversary, Squires finally revealed most (if not all) of his training secrets in *Speed with Endurance*, cowritten by Bruce Lehane. Also, Rodgers appeared on a sports card when the Upper Deck Company released its 2009 Goodwin Champions card set.

Outside of competition, the GBTC family suffered great loss this decade. In 2001, permanent 300-yard masters record-holder Siegel-Davis died of cancer. The following year, Palmer died of a heart attack after a run at the age of forty-eight. In 2004, Bradley died of dehydration on a hot run in the Grand Canyon at the age of twenty-four (she is recognized with the joint Chicago's Universal Sole Club/GBTC annual Margaret L. Bradley Award). Four years later, at the age of twenty-nine, Margaret Nervegna died of brain cancer. And in the following decade, Keith Francis, who, at the time of his death in 2011, held the club record in the 800, died after a long illness at fifty-six. GBTC had unfortunately grappled with loss earlier, including in 1987, when Lonni Stern died of cancer at the age of twenty-eight, and in 1994, when James "Jay" Boviard III died at thirty-six of a brain tumor. GBTC started a savings bond fund for his children and also stitched together a quilt of shirts from races he had run.

Chapter Five

2010–2013

In its fifth decade, the GBTC saw two presidential records established when Bruce Davie became the longest-serving president at six years (2005–10) and Hayden became the first female president (2011). "Being the first female club president was an honor. GBTC has a rich history and I'm so proud to be part of contributing to that history," she said. "I received support and collaboration from [Derderian, Callum and the board] and found the people who compose the track club to be amazingly generous in spirit and time." Callum, in particular, organized GBTC's sprinters, jumpers and throwers, in a way not previously fulfilled.

GBTC reassessed its athletic standards in relation to its tiered system of financial-, travel- and clothing-support allotment. This harkened back to the beginning, when "it was a very narrow mission," noted Mark Duggan, who was involved in the early standard/disbursement policy in 1978. "Give places for high-quality, post-collegiate athletes to continue their career in track. There were other places you could go if you wanted to be a road-runner dominating the road-race circuit." As a result, in mid-2010, a revamped two-tier event standard was instituted.

Individual national champion honors via USATF National Club Track and Field Championship wins came in 2010, from Cotto (110-meter hurdles), Jessica Klett (400-meter hurdles), Alexander (TJ) and Casey Taylor (LJ); in 2011, from Laine (TJ) and Rita Ciambra (PV); and in 2012, from Ruben Sanca (10,000), Daniel Colina (javelin) and Lisa Wilson (discus). At the 2012 USATF East Region outdoor, Laine (TJ) and Alexander (TJ) won. And McCabe in the VISA Championship Series at the 2010 USATF indoors in New Mexico was fourteenth in the 1,500 (4:46.39).

"Qualifying for the VISA championship at the New England championship was a real confidence booster and a milestone for me," said McCabe. "When I entered the race, I wasn't thinking about qualifying. My last two races had been terrible, and I hadn't run a personal record in a long time. I told myself that I had to relax and stay in the moment. I tried not to overthink the race and not focus so much on splits. Everything went smoothly. I had done better than I imagined, which gave me new hope." Not so at VISA. "I did not race well. I had to take three planes to get there. I remember being extremely tired. I was also very stressed. I didn't have a positive experience."

GBTC in this decade's first few years won all twelve New England titles it could with sweeps in the men's and women's indoors and outdoors. Additionally, GBTC won the women's road-racing Grand Prix and the men's and women's cross-country Grand Prix. Subsequently, at the 2011 USATF-NE annual banquet, GBTC earned the inaugural USATF-NE Club of the Year Award. The following year, Derderian was elected USATF-NE president, alongside Victoria Barnaby as vice-president and Will Feldman as an athlete representative.

In the 2010 NU Solomon Invitational 1,500, the top four finishers were (from left) Hannah Hastings (fourth), Jenny Gardynski (third), Laura Hayden (second), Victoria Barnaby (first). *GreaterSnap photo courtesy GBTC.*

GBTC athletes. *Front row, from left:* Jane-Marie Ovanin, Gretchen Chick, Tara (Vance) Womack; *standing:* Kyle Linn MacQueen Feldman, Allison McCabe, Meghan Lynch, Jennifer Lee, Elizabeth Kelly. *GreaterSnap photo, courtesy GBTC.*

USATF-NE indoor wins came in 2010, from Hafiz Greigre (200), McCabe (1500), Dacia Taylor-Samuels (200), men's 4 x 440-yard, men's team and women's team; in 2011, from Alexander Engel (400), McCabe (mile), Harlow (HJ), men's 4 x 440-yard and women's DMR; in 2012 from Engel (400), Tim Bayley (800), Sheldon Allen (60-meter hurdles), Corey Fairfield (HJ), Nicholas Ricciardi (LJ), Nate Hunter (SP), Klett (800), Kyle Linn MacQueen Feldman (mile), Andrea Walkonen (5,000), men's DMR and women's DMR; and in 2013 from Mark Williamson (400) and men's 4 x 440-yard.

USATF-NE outdoor wins came in 2010 from Terrance Young (LJ), Harlow (200), Josette Pierre-Louis (400), Klett (400-meter hurdles), Wilson (SP), Stacey Connor (discus), men's team and women's team; in 2011 from Zach Traina (100), Engel (400), Brad Mish (10,000), Francis Shen (400-meter hurdles), Chris Flynn (TJ), Klett (400-meter hurdles), Victoria Barnaby (3000-meter steeplechase), Harlow (HJ), Ciambra (PV) and men's 4 x 100; and in 2012 from David Kennedy (100), Greigre (200), Christian Tirella (400), Brian Freitas (400-meter hurdles), Flynn (TJ), Hunter (SP), Richard McNeil (discus), Taylor-Samuels (100, 200, LJ), Klett (400), McCabe (800),

MacQueen Feldman (1500, 5000), Connor (SP, discus), men's 4 x 100, men's 4 x 400, women's 4 x 100 and women's 4 x 400. Anecdotally, Victoria Barnaby at the 2012 GBTC Invitational sang the National Anthem.

MacQueen Feldman, in particular, set records in the 1,500, mile and 3,000 (twice in three weeks) in 2012, "a tremendous year for me. It was the first time I ran a full indoor and outdoor track schedule in nearly a decade. I honestly was never trying to break club records, but as my fitness improved, I became more aware of what they were and knew that I may have the potential to break them." The first 3,000 fell at BU. "I was overwhelmed with excitement, but also fear," she recalled after successfully pleading to be reassigned to the fast heat. "Eventually, two packs formed—the lead pack and the chase pack. I was hanging on at the back of the chase pack.

I panicked for a second but reminded myself that I wasn't feeling uncomfortable and that I just needed to stay put but to also be aware of what was happening at the front of the pack. I ended up passing several people during the next few laps." She broke her own record at Columbia, and then forty-one weeks later, McCabe broke it at the 2012 BU Mini Meet #1 in 9:32.18.

"I knew I was in good cross-country shape," said McCabe. "I hadn't run a 3K in a few years, so I wasn't too sure how it would feel. I was very relaxed going in. I wanted to go out conservatively, especially in the first few laps. I just wanted to run how I felt. Everything went as planned. I felt comfortable the whole way. I was surprised at how good I still felt at the bell lap. I was happy that after three stress fractures, I was

With support from fellow teammates Victoria Barnaby (6) and Jenny Cunningham (21) at the 2012 BU Mini Meet #1, Allison McCabe (76) sets the club record in the 3,000. *Ryan Irwin photo courtesy GBTC.*

able to come back and run a PR so early in the track season. It made all those pool workouts worth it."

The women won the 2010 USATF-NE Grand Prix with a second-pace showing at the Bay State Marathon with Marybeth Baxter, Zandra Walton and Johnson. In master's action, Lawson won 400 silver and 4 x 200 gold at the 2010 World Master's Indoor Athletics Championships in Canada, and at the 2010 USATF Master's indoors, gold went to Everad Samuels, Sean Earle, Harrison, Christine Kloiber and men's 4 x 400 (Cahill, Jim Watts, non-GBTC recruit Rodney Zook and Callum), and bronze to Wayne Burwell, Cahill, Samuels and Lawson.

GBTC continued to field teams at various harrier meets, including every USATF National Club Cross-Country Championship. In 2012, joining other club-sponsored events was the newly named GBTC Cross-Country Invitational, formerly the Bradley Palmer Cross-Country Club Challenge and Topsfield Cross-Country Festival, which Sara Donahue won in 2010. She had also run a 2:46:17 for sixty-ninth place at the 2008 U.S. Olympic Trials women's marathon in Boston.

At the 2010 Ronald McDonald House of Providence Women's Classic Amgen 5K. *From left*: Jennifer Lee, Ronnesia Gaskins, Sara Donahue, Gretchen Chick, Meghan Lynch, Allison McCabe, Katie Fobert, Scarlett Graham, Anna Novick, Jenny Gardynski. *Photo by Tom Derderian.*

At the 2011 Chicago Marathon, while the goal for MacQueen Feldman wasn't necessarily the overall victory, her aim was still high. "I was a 3:03 marathoner shooting for a 2012 Olympic Trials Qualifier," she said, referring to the 2:46 standard. "I don't think anyone believed I would come close. Many said just breaking three hours is tough to do. But I worked my butt off for three straight months to give myself a good shot. I did fall short (2:49:14), but not by much. It really helped me to see that putting in the hard work, consistent training and believing in yourself are keys to success in this sport."

GBTC won team titles at the 2010 Amgen 5K (Gretchen Chick, Donahue, Anna Novick, McCabe and Lee) and the Cape Cod Marathon relay with Margaret's Mixed Up Fish (2010–11), Margaret Bradley's Fish (2010–12) and Margaret's Fisherman (2012).

Internationally for GBTC, Jamaica's Riettie competed in the 2010 CACC, Pan American Games and Commonwealth Games; Puerto Rico's Cotto medaled in the 2010–11 CACC, 2010 Central American and Caribbean Games (CACG) and 2010 and 2012 Ibero-American Championships and

At his eightieth birthday party in 2012. *From left*: new octogenarian Bill Squires celebrates with Bill Rodgers, Gina Fiandaca, Paul Caruccio. *Photo by Paul C. Clerici.*

competed in the 2012 Olympics; Cape Verdi's Sanca competed in the 2012 Ibero-American Championships; Haiti's Laine won gold at the 2011 CACG and competed in the 2012 Olympics; Trinidad and Tobago's Alexander medaled at the 2010 CACG, Commonwealth Games and 2011 CACC and competed in the 2012 Olympics.

In November 2012, Squires turned eighty and was feted in style at BC in an afternoon-long public showing of support and appreciation. After being born with a late-diagnosed defective heart valve and surviving heart attacks, a stroke, stents and a pacemaker, he was genuinely touched by the outpouring of accolades and presentations.

Jack McDonald was especially moved with the opportunity: "All along, my relationship with Coach went from coach-athlete to almost father-son-like. Because I was a fatherless guy, I latched onto Coach more than probably he knew. My mother remarried and all that, but just in terms of the sports and that he basically said to me to go back to school, get my degree, get my master's. He didn't know how much I looked up to him."

Continuing under coaches Callum, Derderian and Rod Hemingway and a healthy treasury and membership body, GBTC's future beholds promise. At the 2013 USATF National Youth indoors, for instance, Milton Academy senior Ben Bosworth won the 1,500 (MR 4:16.40): "It's always cool to win, but especially so when there are so many people watching. I really feel that I am associated with one of the premier track clubs in the world. I really like the fact that the team welcomed me to their ranks without blinking an eye at my age. I really respect the history of the club and am humbled by the talent it boasts of, past and present."

Alberto Salazar (left) and Fred Doyle were honored at the 2009 Independent Running Retailers Association (IRRA) the Running Specialty Hall of Fame induction ceremony. *Courtesy Fred Doyle.*

Fred Doyle emcees the Saucony Cheers to Boston Running event, which saluted, among others, (sitting, from left) Tommy Leonard, Bob Sevene and Bill Squires. *Photo by Paul C. Clerici.*

The original Rookie, Salazar, looked back at his GBTC days and noted, "Coach Squires and the GBTC taught me to take a long-term approach with running. It's something I've never forgotten and is a key component of whatever success I've had as a coach. I owe the most to these guys from the GBTC: Coach Squires, for making me into the runner I became; Kirk Pfrangle, for mentoring me in life and running; and Mark Duggan and Randy Thomas, for taking me under their wings and pushing me in workouts. All of them helped me out of the kindness of their hearts, and now I feel it's my turn to pass it on to others."

As a forty-year-old in 2013, GBTC treated itself to a website makeover and further embraced the times with the introduction of a Facebook page, Twitter account and blogs. And members are still in demand on the bookshelves, as Rodgers and Salazar—after publishing several training books—released autobiographies and were both heavily featured in another running book.

In recognition of GBTC's anniversary, during the 2013 Boston Marathon Weekend at a special evening-long event called Cheers to Boston Running,

Saucony saluted the club in a packed house of fans, Boston champions and dozens of club members. And then three days later on Patriots' Day, the GBTC family, the running community and the world joined together in the aftermath of unthinkable horror when two sidewalk bombs within blocks of the Boston Marathon finish line (the second bomb exploded five hundred feet beyond mile twenty-six) tragically took lives and innocence and forced officials to stop the race with just over 5,700 runners still on the course.

GBTC's Gary Circosta was one of the last runners to cross the finish line, just two minutes prior to the first detonation. "My wife and daughter always stand at the twenty-six-mile marker to watch for me. I ran by them literally smiling ear-to-ear! I just passed the explosion site before the blast," recalled the sixty-six-year-old, whose 4:07:09 was close enough to the bursts that only 607 more runners behind him were recorded before cessation. "As usual [after I pass my family], they then immediately left the area to go to the family reunion area. Fortunately for my family, we were all safe. Can you imagine my agony if I were three minutes slower! It went from the best of days to the worst of days in a matter of moments. I sincerely mourn for all the victims."

At the Saucony Cheers to Boston Running event that saluted GBTC, honored guests included, *from left*: Bill Clark, Don Ricciato, Bill Squires, Bob Hodge, Fred Doyle, Tommy Leonard, Gary Wallace, Randy Thomas, Mike Roche, Mark Duggan, Bob Sevene and Dick Mahoney. *Photo by Paul C. Clerici.*

A gathering of GBTC alums. *From left*: Greg Meyer, Bob Hodge, Dick Mahoney, Bill Squires, Alberto Salazar, Brad Hurst and Vinnie Fleming. *Photo by Paul C. Clerici.*

With over thirty members running Boston, GBTC president John Raguin's concern was for their safety. "We used Facebook as the main vehicle to find out where people were. Everyone posted up who they had seen after the explosions to make sure that we had everyone accounted for. It took well into the evening for everyone to post up, but everyone did."

On the docket forty years and a day after the club's very formation was scheduled another get-together of running royalty. This time, the celebration recognized not only those involved in the club but also the club itself. "I am truly honored to be president of GBTC, let alone during the fortieth-anniversary year," said Raguin. "In my view, GBTC is the most storied running club in the entire country. GBTC has helped over two thousand athletes over the years. It has consistently fielded competitive teams in not only track and field but also road races and cross-country. I think it's important to note how many athletes that GBTC has helped over the years to take their running to the next level. I think this is really the legacy that GBTC leaves behind as well as brings forward to the future."

To that point, the lineage indeed continues in Squires-coached athletes—including Salazar, who coaches Olympic medalists Mo Farah and Galen Rupp; Derderian, who coaches GBTC; Thomas, who coaches at BC; and Sevene, who coached six-time Northeast Conference Coach of the Year Mike Toomey of Endicott College and five-time Big Ten Coach of the Year Steve Plasencia of the University of Minnesota. "The success I have had is a direct result of my early days with the GBTC and being in Bill's space as both an athlete and a friend," said Sevene. "Bill had the most influence on me and my coaching philosophy during my forty-three years of coaching. Bill Squires's philosophy was way ahead of his time and has become a cornerstone on the success of the coaching greats today. Bill's distance training is a complement to the track work and the speed and [the] amount a direct relationship [is] to the intensity of the track training and the ability of the athlete to handle the workload."

GBTC is also more than just a club, to wit Papadopoulos attested of his time in the United States. "I'll never forget how my teammates organized the 'Ioannis America' series when I told them I had to return to Greece because of the expiration of my visa. That was a part of the American-themed events that I had to attend with them. It was a sort of cultural orientation that included drive-in cinemas, minor league hockey games, a Thanksgiving dinner at springtime and attending a Red Sox game. To me, it was a family."

Dillon recalled the time he left PC and joined GBTC, only to return and graduate: "My running was improving steadily and I felt if I could find the right coach and training partners, I'd be able to make the next step while I figured out for sure what I wanted to do. One day, Coach Squires pulled me aside after one of these [struggling] workouts. He said, 'Look, Dan. You have more talent than I think you even realize. Don't rush it. And most of all, don't get too comfortable here with GBTC. I like having you here, and I want to help you; but I would rather that you get back down to Providence and finish school.' I knew that Coach was really looking out for what was right for me over the long haul."

Doyle recalled when at the 1980 U.S. Olympic Trials Marathon, he heard runners agonizing over their performance. "Some were saying they work only four hours, their wives were working two jobs—they risked everything. They put their whole lives in this. But we got great advice from the master. Squires would tell us it's an enjoyable sport, but get a job, get a career, get an education. I credit him for that."

Willard's always been grateful, stating, "I am very thankful to the GBTC for inviting me into its ranks, even for such a short time. It was a time in my life that I look back on and remember gritty competition, but mostly good times shared with new friends."

Above, fom left: Fred Doyle, Bill Squires, Mark Duggan. *Photo by Paul C. Clerici.*

Left: Bill Rodgers (left) and Greg Meyer. *Photo by Paul C. Clerici.*

A GBTC-themed wedding cake topper. *Courtesy Kyle Linn MacQueen Feldman and Will Feldman.*

(Meade) Lavelle looked back and recalls, "My running years were some of the best times of my life. My husband, TL, and I made a lot of friends during these years and enjoyed all aspects of the running scene. Running with the other women from the club on a weekly basis for our hill and track workouts was also key to my improvements when it came to race day. It was a total blast!"

Egbor equally appreciated wearing the club red, saying, "I ran in college for a small school. I was usually the single runner or the single very good runner. Coming to GBTC, I was one of many very, very good runners. We had a swagger that we could win track meets as a team, not just individual wins. I love my individual wins, and I will not trade them; but it felt really good to be part of a club that won as a team."

Meyer—whose 1983 Boston win as the most recent American marked its thirtieth anniversary the same year GBTC celebrated its fortieth—fondly recalled the cachet that traveled with the club. "When we would show up at a race, people would look at us and say, 'Shit! Greater Boston's here. We're screwed.' That's a fun thing," he smiled. "And [we] earned it."

Index

A

Abeguile, Elaine 94
Adams, Gillian 87
Alemu, Kifle 94
Alexander, Ayanna 100, 103, 109, 115
Allen, Sheldon 111
Amoscato, Barb 85

B

Badea, Claudio 92
Ball, Cathy 83, 84
Barnaby, Bob 46
Barnaby, Victoria 110, 111, 112
Barnett, Posie 82
Barrett, Deon 93, 94
Bateman, James 102
Baxter, Marybeth 113
Bayi, Filbert 39
Bayley, Tim 111
Bedoya, David 103
Bergh, Sue 94
Berit, Jon 82, 83, 88, 90, 96
Bernard, Joan 91

Bickford, Bruce 36, 52, 61, 65, 69, 88
Binkley, Aaron 102
Bjorklund, Garry 40, 43
Blake, Jessica 103, 107
Blouin, John 93, 94
Bohlke, Joan 100
Bond, Bruce 95
Bonstelle, Christy 102
Bosworth, Ben 115
Boviard, James "Jay," III 108
Bradley, Margaret 107, 108, 114
Bray, Mary Ann 58, 68, 72, 81, 82
Brommer Duquette, Lois 89, 90, 91, 95
Browne, Eamonn 92
Brzostowski, Barbara 85
Burfoot, Ambrose "Amby" 22, 80
Burwell, Wayne 113

C

Cahill, Dave 102, 106, 113

Calder, Steve 34
Callahan, Don 84
Callum, David 104, 106, 109, 113, 115
Carrancho, Michelle 100
Carter, President Jimmy 54, 63
Caruccio, Paul 69
Catalano, Patti (Lyons) 80
Chaggaris, Maegan 103
Champion, Margaret 58
Cheema, Moeen 93
Chesto, Joe 86
Chick, Gretchen 114
Ciambra, Rita 109, 111
Cipelle, Wendy 92, 95
Ciraface, Peter 69
Circosta, Gary 117
Clare, Tessa 102
Clark, Bill 69
Clark, Nancy 86, 91
Clayton, Robin 68
Clifford, Bob 80, 82, 86, 89, 90, 108
Clinton, President Bill 49, 54
Colina, Daniel 109

Colon, Andie 102
Conboy, Lisa 92
Concannon, Joe 71, 97
Conkin, Deke 102
Connor, Stacey 111
Cornelius, Lynn 90, 91
Cotto, Hector 102, 103, 109, 114
Coverdale, Miles 69
Cowens, Dave 58
Crain, Ethan 94
Crouse, Karen 95, 108
Crowley, Joe 26
Cruz, J.R. 103
Cullina, Jane 100
Cully, Wendy 59

D

Darley, Jesse 94, 95
Dauphin, Cynthia 75
Davie, Bruce 109
DeGrande, Francine 68
Delany, John 108
Demers, John 61
Dendy, Joyce 94
Deprospo, Norma 73
Derderian, Tom 24, 26, 52, 68, 86, 87, 95, 97, 98, 103, 104, 108, 109, 110, 115, 119
Dickinson, Diana 58, 68
Diehl, Charlie 15
Dillon, Dan 27, 43, 45, 47, 50, 51, 56, 61, 65, 69, 80, 119
DiMascio, Marianne 90
Doherty, Mike 44
Doherty, Pat 44
Doherty, Tim 44
Doherty, Tom 44
Donahue, Sara 113, 114
Donohoe Hussey, Julie 90, 92, 94
Donovan, Paula 107

Donovan, Tim 50, 69, 71, 76
Doyle, Fred 22, 30, 37, 40, 43, 46, 47, 50, 60, 64, 65, 70, 73, 75, 76, 97, 119
Drayton, Jerome 43
Duckworth, Pam 58, 68, 72, 73, 82, 89, 90, 91, 108
Duggan, Charlie 37
Duggan, Mark 30, 34, 37, 40, 46, 47, 52, 59, 69, 70, 109, 116
Dulong, Art 37
Dunn, Leo 22
Duquette, Ralph 89, 90
Durkin, Jim 79
Dyer, Rip 65

E

Earle, Sean 113
Egbor, Stanley 99, 103, 104, 122
Elliott, Dave 15, 21, 22, 24, 27
Ellis, Jon 102
Engel, Alexander 111
Engle, Troy 75
Ezersky, Dave 52
Ezersky, Patricia 84

F

Facey, Don 42, 43, 59
Fairfield, Corey 111
Feldman, Will 110
Fenton, Mark 75, 82
Fikel, Lori 83
Fine, Dotty 70, 73
Finlay, Caroline 100
Fisher, Wayne 93
Fleming, Vinnie "Vin" 16, 26, 30, 34, 43, 44,

45, 52, 56, 69, 71, 77, 80
Flynn, Chris 111
Francis, Keith 61, 108
Frank, Lisa 95
Freitas, Brian 111
Fultz, Jack 43, 48, 49
Furey, Sean 100, 102

G

Galloway, Jeff 22, 23
Gavenda, Lauri 94
Gedritis, Mary Ann 72
Gilligan, Bill 21
Gilligan, Sharon (O'Hagan) 58, 72, 73, 79, 82, 83, 89, 91
Gilligan, Thom 46, 54, 55, 70, 75, 76, 80, 82, 89
Gillin, Bill 50
Goldszer, Bob 69
Gradhand, Ulrike 100
Graham, Scott 26, 30, 37, 47, 69
Grant, Natalie 100
Gregorek, John 35
Greigre, Hafiz 111
Grilk, Tom 40, 42, 43, 53, 55, 59, 97
Guerrini, Tom 95

H

Hagmeier, Mike 83
Hague, Jim 86
Halberstadt, Johnny 82
Hall, Bob 30, 31, 34, 62, 71
Harlow, Jennifer 102, 111
Haro, Mariano 28
Harrison, Richard 102, 113

Hastings, Cynthia 68, 72, 73, 82, 87, 94
Hayden, Laura 100, 107, 109
Haynes, Mike 85
Hebert, Jim 76, 82, 85
Heffernan, John 98
Hensley, Bob 47
Henson, Art 102
Hewitt, Jason 102
Hicks, Kevin 88
Hodge, Bob 8, 20, 26, 30, 34, 36, 37, 40, 43, 44, 47, 50, 51, 52, 53, 54, 56, 61, 64, 65, 71, 80, 97
Hodge, Frannie (Fisher) 58, 68, 72, 73, 82, 83
Hogan, Rick 81
Hopkins, Pete 86
Horovitz, Israel 86, 87
Huber, Bridgette 68
Hunter, Nate 111
Hurst, Brad 75, 76
Hussey, Chris 90, 91

J

Jack, Johann 93, 99, 103, 104
Jadotte, Joeanne 102
Jankowski, Ann Marie 84
Jennings, Lynn 43, 97
Jessup, Hubert "Hugh" 95, 108
Johnson, Lynn 103, 113
Jones, Sharpless 34
Jones, Steve 88
Junger, Sebastian 80, 84, 86, 90

K

Kandamar, Erin (Cullinane) 94, 106
Kardong, Don 43

Kehoe, Jason 89
Kelley, Johnny "the Elder" 97
Kelley, Johnny "the Younger" 80
Kennedy, Sen. Edward 60
Keyes, Steve 102
King, Ann 95
Klett, Jessica 109, 111
Kloiber, Christine 113
Krise, Raymond 69, 86

L

Laine, Samyr 100, 102, 109, 115
Lane, Chris 15, 16
Lavelle, Pat (Meade) 71, 72, 81, 82, 121
Lavelle, Tom "TL" 72
Lawson, Sarah 100, 102, 106, 113
Leach, Audrey 83, 84
Lecoq, Linda 58
Lee, Jennifer 100
Lehane, Bruce 108
Leonard, Tommy 35, 42, 59, 60, 77, 80, 97
Lettis, Paula 68, 69
Ligor, Norma 58, 72
Lindsay, Herb 65
Liquori, Marty 26, 35, 38
Lupica, Sue 58, 59, 82
Lydiard, Arthur 104
Lynch, Pat 43

M

MacQueen Feldman, Kyle Linn 111, 112, 114
Macri, Sandy 68
Mahan, Tom 65
Mahoney, Dick 8, 15, 16, 26, 30, 34, 35, 37, 40, 52, 53, 56, 64, 68, 69, 70, 71, 80, 84, 97

Mahoney, Maura 93
Manolatou, Christina 93, 94
Matar, Rania 108
Mattocks, Kristin 95
Mays, Glen 94, 103
McAllister, Scott 42
McArdle, Colin 102
McCabe, Allison 102, 110, 111, 112, 114
McCallum, Bob 47
McDonald, Jack 13, 14, 15, 16, 17, 18, 21, 22, 26, 27, 34, 37, 38, 39, 40, 42, 56, 115
McDonald, Kay 91
McDonald, Maura 94
McGill, Janet 90
McGillivray, Dave 42, 46, 49, 55, 61, 63
McGrath, John 43, 59, 69, 71
McGuirl, John 92
McManus, Claire 90, 95
McNamara, John 84, 86
McNeil, Richard 111
Merritt, Kim 43
Meyer, Greg 36, 53, 55, 56, 68, 79
Miami, Lou 85
Milld, Alan 16
Miller, Sandy 58, 72, 91, 93
Miller, Todd 42
Mish, Brad 111
Mitchell, Jan 69, 72
Moore, Brian 102
Moore, Meg Mitchell 86
Morris, Joanne 91
Murdock, Bob 84, 86, 90
Murphy, Walter 30

N

Neckas, Rick 37

Nehiley, Shawna 94
Nelson, Barbara 91
Nephew, Ben 103, 104
Nervegna, Margaret 108
Newman, Larry 59, 73, 74, 89, 97
Newsham, Bill 91, 92, 95, 106
Nichols, Rich 61
Nickerson, Dick 95
Nickerson, John 91
Novick, Anna 114

O

Obama, President Barack 63
O'Brien, Jim 22, 70, 74, 106
O'Brien, Sara 100, 102
Occean, Caroline 100, 102
O'Connell, Mike "the Tyke" 76
O'Donovan, Kerry 94
Okerman, Bill 70, 74, 76
O'Leary, Jim 95
Olson, Dan 100
O'Neill, Terry 93, 106
Oparowski, Paul 47, 48, 64

P

Palmer, Andy 70, 79, 80, 108
Papadopoulos, Ioannis 86, 103, 104, 107, 119
Parekh, Payal 94
Parker, Andrew 93
Parks, Michelle 95
Parrotta, Domenic 91
Patrick, Claudia 91
Pawlicki, Jim 93, 94, 95
Pearson, Rodney 43, 75, 76, 86

Pease, Ben 93
Peterson, Jim 39
Petitto, Rocco 47
Pfitzinger, Pete 52, 65, 66, 70, 86
Pfrangle, Kirk 15, 16, 17, 25, 39, 46, 97, 116
Phelan, Rosemary 94
Pierre-Louis, Josette 111
Pillay, Geraldine 103
Pistone, John 15, 17
Powell, Kelly 100
Prefontaine, Steve "Pre" 30, 38
Prepetit, Serge 92
Pruitt, Judy 91
Puckerin, Rich 61
Putnam, Stephen 102

R

Radzevich, Vic 102
Raguin, John 118
Rapaport, Jennifer 94
Rasp, Maureen 72
Rattray, Karen 90, 91
Reardon, Jim 94
Reavis, Toni 89
Reed, George 47, 48
Reed, Monica 68, 72
Reeder, Mark 93
Regan, Catherine 100
Reid, Pershing 92, 93
Reilly, Brendan 82
Reytblat, Mark 74
Ricciardi, Nicholas 111
Ricciato, Don 15, 16, 17, 20, 21, 22, 27, 30
Richardson, Tom 95
Riettie, Kateema 100, 102, 103, 114
Roberts, Sherry 84
Roche, Mike 36, 46, 55, 65, 70
Rodgers, Bill 8, 16, 20, 22, 23, 24, 26, 28, 29,

30, 31, 32, 34, 35, 36, 37, 40, 42, 43, 44, 45, 46, 47, 48, 49, 51, 52, 53, 54, 55, 56, 60, 63, 64, 65, 68, 69, 70, 71, 77, 79, 80, 82, 83, 86, 88, 97, 108, 116
Romero, Cesar 85
Romvos, Judy 91
Rowe Salem, Amory 93, 94
Russell, Kevin 92, 98
Ryan, Kevin 35, 80
Ryun, Jim 38

S

Salazar, Alberto 27, 30, 34, 35, 36, 37, 51, 56, 65, 69, 71, 79, 83, 86, 88, 108, 116, 118
Saltalamacchia, Cathy 84
Samuels, Everad 113
Samuelson, Joan Benoit 54, 80
Sanca, Rubin 109, 115
Sauer, Barbara 83, 89, 91
Schmitt, Dianne 72
Scott, Steve 35, 51
Seeherman, Josh 102, 106
Semple, John "Jock" 22, 24, 30
Sevene, Bob 15, 17, 20, 21, 24, 25, 27, 30, 32, 42, 56, 59, 70, 77, 97, 119
Shams, Nastaran 100, 102
Shanor, Rachel 91, 92
Shen, Frances 111
Shorter, Frank 22, 35, 40, 43, 51, 56, 107
Siegel-Davis, Elydia 68, 108
Siegrist, Sloan 100, 103

Simpson, Chris 102, 106
Smith, Geoff 97
Smith, Jean 72, 73, 81, 82,
    83, 90, 91, 95
Smith, Tracy 30
Smith, William "Billy"
    17, 25
Snyder, Gary 106
Sparks, Lori 58
Spolidoro, Julie 93
Squires, Bill 8, 11, 15, 16,
    17, 18, 20, 22, 23,
    24, 25, 26, 27, 28,
    29, 30, 31, 32, 35,
    36, 37, 38, 39, 40,
    43, 45, 46, 48, 50,
    51, 52, 53, 54, 55,
    56, 57, 58, 59, 63,
    64, 69, 70, 71, 77,
    79, 80, 83, 86, 97,
    98, 103, 104, 108,
    115, 116, 118, 119
Stern, Lonni 108
Stevens, Marzuki 100
Stewart, Ian 28
Stewart, Jimmy 85
Stumpf, Susan 76
Subin, Keely 100
Sun, Maria 93

T

Taylor, Casey 109
Taylor-Samuels, Dacia
    111
Thomas, Randy 8, 30,
    35, 46, 51, 56,
    116, 119
Tirella, Christian 111
Tompkins, Mark 94
Traina, Zach 111
Trainor, Kourtney 100
Traiser, Marty 85, 86
Treacy, John 47, 50
Treseler, Fred 42
Tucker, Eric 108

Turmala, Michael 98
Tuttle, Gary 28
Tuttle, Mark 98

U

Urich, Robert 85

V

Vaitones, Steve 75, 79
Veltri, Joanna 94, 98, 106
Vieweg, Kathy 72
Viren, Lasse 87
Virgin, Craig 30, 36, 65

W

Wagner, Robert 85
Walker, John 39
Walkonen, Andrea 111
Wallace, Gary 47, 64, 66,
    71, 75, 76, 83
Walton, Zandra 113
Ward, Bob 105, 106
Watts, Jim 113
Welch, Joe 100
Wells, Kit 103
Willard, Anna 100,
    102, 119
Williams, Livvy 93, 94
Williams, Sherita 100, 104
Williamson, Mark 111
Wilson, Lisa 109, 111
Wiseman, Susan 94
Wohlhuter, Rick 24
Womack, Andrew 103
Womack, Tara (Vance)
    103

Y

Young, Mark 22
Young, Terrance 111

Z

Zook, Rodney 113

About the Author

Paul C. Clerici is a freelance journalist, writer, photographer and former newspaper and sports editor who has been recognized in the *Who's Who in the East* publication. He has written for the *Foxboro Reporter*, the *Walpole Times*, *Boston College Chronicle*, *New England Patriots Weekly*, *New England Runner*, *North End* magazine, *Orlando Attractions* magazine, *Running Times* and *State Street Journal* and has produced shows at Walpole Community Television, where he is on the board of directors. A New England and Massachusetts press associations award winner, he is also a regular contributor to *Marathon & Beyond* magazine. The race director of the Camy 5K Run & David 5K Walk, he has competed in nearly every distance from the mile to the marathon—including two triathlons and forty-three marathons, of which twenty-three were the Boston Marathon in consecutive years—and has won several age-group and Clydesdale awards. A graduate of Curry College, the Walpole High School Hall of Fame member resides in his Massachusetts hometown.

Photo by Carol Hunt-Clerici.